JENSON BUTTON

HOW TO BE AN F1 DRIVER

JENSON BUTTON

HOW TO BE AN
F1 DRIVER

BLINK
bringing you closer

Published by Blink Publishing
2.25, The Plaza,
535 Kings Road,
Chelsea Harbour,
London, SW10 0SZ

www.blinkpublishing.co.uk

facebook.com/blinkpublishing
twitter.com/blinkpublishing

Hardback – 978-1-788-702-61-4
Trade paperback – 978-1-788-702-62-1
Ebook – 978-1-788-702-63-8

A CIP catalogue of this book is available from the British Library.

Typeset by seagulls.net
Printed and bound in Great Britain by Clays Ltd, Elcograf S.p.A.

1 3 5 7 9 10 8 6 4 2

Blink Publishing is an imprint of Bonnier Books UK
www.bonnierbooks.co.uk

To the 'new boy', Hendrix.

I'm going to buy you a copy of *How To Be A Doctor*
as well to balance things out.

CONTENTS

DRIVING
LESSONS

'Right, Mr Burton,' says the driving instructor, with the distinctive leathery purr of someone born and bred in Los Angeles.

'It's Button, actually,' I correct him, settling in behind the wheel of the Honda Accord, ready for my lesson. 'Jenson Button.'

'Ginseng Button?'

I try again. 'Jenson Button.'

'Of course!' he explodes. 'It's your English accent. Jenson Button. Jen-son But-ton. Right. Got it. Okay, Mr But-ton, so you're here today so that we can get you up to speed on your LA driving ahead of your test, is that right?'

'Yes,' I reply.

What I've discovered since moving in with Brittny is that making my way around LA isn't simply a case of staying on the right-hand side of the road and hoping for the best. There are tons of little things you need to know, like the fact that you're permitted to turn right at a red stop light, or the odd way you have to deal with cycle lanes, and I need to know all this in order to get my Californian driving licence. It doesn't matter where you're from, or what you do for a living, you need a Californian driving licence if you want to use the roads.

In actual fact, it will turn out that I don't really need to learn this stuff for the test when it eventually happens, because the test consists of me very nervously driving around Fontana for a bit, with the examiner saying, 'It's fifty here, it's fifty, you can go faster,' out of the side of her mouth, and then passing me on all aspects of the test apart from one – braking. I'd braked too late, apparently.

'I didn't brake too late,' I will moan to Brittny afterwards.

'You always brake too late,' she responds, long-sufferingly.

But that's to come. Right now, I just need to get the hang of the road systems in my adopted home of LA, and the best way of doing that is by having an actual driving lesson. On the one hand, this is uncharacteristically sensible of me. On the other hand, I still have the shame of failing my first UK driving test branded on my heart so I want to get it right. Besides, Britt's dad is a Californian Highway Patrol officer so I need to keep my nose clean.

'Okay, Mr But-ton, let's try moving off, shall we?' says the instructor. We get rolling and as we drive it occurs to me that this is only my fourth-ever driving lesson, and there's been a twenty-year gap between this one and the first three, when my instructor was Roger Brunt, who used to race against my dad in autocross. It wasn't Roger's fault that I went on to fail. I was too cocky, that was my problem.

'You're doing well,' the instructor assures me, before asking, 'What is it that you do for a living, Mr But-ton?'

'Actually, I'm a driver,' I tell him.

He's thinking. *Pizza delivery? Uber? UPS?*

'A racing driver,' I add, helpfully.

'A racing driver? Wow,' he says. He lapses into silence but when I steal a glance over at him I can see that he's googling me.

'Wow,' he says at last, holding up the phone. 'Is this you?'

'Yeah,' I say, 'that's me.'

He squints at the phone. 'Says here that you've retired from Form-ula One. Is that right?'

'Well...' I say.

DON'T CALL IT A COMEBACK

Like the song goes, I heard it through the grapevine.

'They're going to call you.'

Various people telling me. *They're going to call you. Any day now.* And I'd be standing by the side of my pool thinking, *Bugger. Really? Maybe I should change my number...*

The problem was that my last race in Formula One (or what I thought at the time would be my last race in Formula One) had been at Abu Dhabi in 2016 and it had been awesome. It wasn't a great race – I'd retired with a broken right front suspension – but in many ways that didn't matter, and probably even improved the situation, because it meant that I'd had my own little farewell before the end, without competing with the podium celebrations (which I would have overshadowed, obviously).

My team was all there, giving it the big goodbye: my friends and family, Brittny, the whole crew. It was a fantastic send-off and no better way to end 17 years in the game, a lifetime spent on planes, in motorhomes and being squeezed into the cockpits of cars. Yes, it was the stuff of boyhood dreams, and no way do I want to give the impression that I'm at all ungrateful about any of that because I spent those 17 years pinching myself at my good fortune, but…

There's always a 'but'. My father had died in 2014, and with him went some of me. Not my passion for racing, which as you're about to find out, has never dimmed. But my taste for the life of Formula One. Without him the paddock hadn't been quite the same. Not only that but I was mentally and physically exhausted – tired of what is, after all, a repetitious life. And there comes a time when, no matter how great it is, you want a break from that repetition. So I'd turned my back on F1 and decided to do something different for a while: take part in triathlons, do a bit of decorating. I wanted to enjoy the freedom from the various pressures of the sport: the teams, the teammates, the sponsors, the media, the whole brilliant but physically and emotionally exhausting merry-go-round of it all. For the first time in my adult life my home was more than a crash pad; I was starting to think of putting down roots, and in Brittny I'd met someone with whom I wanted to share that experience, who maybe was the catalyst for it all. I'd even earned my Californian driving licence, and I was shortly to be scratching my racing itch by competing in Super GT.

In other words, my ducks were in a row.

And F1 did not feature.

Hey, I thought. *Maybe the grapevine is wrong on this occasion. Perhaps the call will never come.*

And then the phone went one morning and it was McLaren principal Eric Boullier, who told me that Fernando Alonso wanted to go off and drive the Indianapolis 500, which was taking place on the very same day as the 2017 Monaco Grand Prix, which meant that...

'I want you to come and race at Monaco in May.'

It was the beginning of April, so I was like, 'But I haven't driven the car. I haven't done any racing since November last year. I've been out here training for triathlons and decorating. If you need advice on what shade to paint your wall, I'm your man, but chucking me in at Monaco...?'

The thing is that as a racing driver, it doesn't matter what you drive, you want to be prepared because you still care what people think, and I was well aware that the season had featured one of the sport's biggest-ever rule changes. The car would be a completely different animal. Not just a new chassis but bigger tyres, heavier, wider, and with more downforce.

'You're the reserve driver,' Eric pointed out in the face of my obvious reluctance, 'this is your job.'

'Oh okay. Um, let me have a think.'

I was stalling. Eric and I both knew that I was contractually obliged to drive. Even so, I looked at my pool. I thought about Brittny, who was pottering about in the house somewhere, and I called Richard Goddard, my manager. 'Can I get out of this?'

He cleared his throat. 'Well, not really, no. I mean, they're paying you a lot of money to basically do nothing this year apart from be on call in case they need you.'

'Yeah, but I didn't think they'd need me.'

'Well, they do, Jenson. They want you to drive their Formula One car in probably the world's most prestigious Grand Prix. Hard life, isn't it?'

Richard knows about as much about being a racing driver as I know about managing racing drivers. Which is to say, quite a lot, actually, and certainly much more than the ordinary Joe. But still not the full enchilada. What's it like to sit behind the wheel of a racing car? How does it feel to be a part of the Grand Prix circus? The kit, the clobber? The rituals, rules and rivalries? How to take a corner, how to run a motorhome and why you should never, under any circumstance, buy a yacht.

All the stuff you're about to find out, in fact – assuming you read on.

Anyway. I got the picture, ended the call and had a quick word with myself. A couple of minutes was all it took, and when I rang back it was with a revised approach. 'Cheers, Eric,' I said, 'I'm really excited to be racing for you again.'

And I meant it, I really did, because my philosophy in life is that when you set out to do something, whatever it is, you have to do it properly.

Especially when you're contractually obliged to do so.

MONACO

Years ago, when Lewis was my teammate at McLaren, the two of us did voiceovers for an animated series called *Tooned* in which we played ourselves. It was my second foray into the world of quality drama after an Oscar-winning Head & Shoulders ad I did in 2011, and I thought it was pretty good, actually, and certainly something to show the kids one day.

Anyway, *Tooned* featured a large underground track that the cartoon Lewis and I used for practice, and because of that a lot of people assumed that such a thing really existed at McLaren HQ in Woking.

Reality flash: it didn't.

What we did have, however, was a simulator – and that became my home for two days prior to the race. Actually, the car felt all right. I began to wonder if I was worrying about nothing. True, I rolled it into the harbour. Twice. But I reassured myself that it couldn't happen in real life thanks to the barriers, and felt that the overall experience was pretty positive.

Next thing you know, I was arriving at the circuit. Like Hannibal in *The A-Team*, I had assembled my old crew – and I didn't even have to disguise myself as 'Mr Lee, the dry cleaner'. With me came Brittny, Richard, my physio Mikey, my best mate Chrissy Buncombe, my PR guy James Williamson – all the old faces.

Even so, walking into the paddock was strange. What struck me was a sense that things were unchanged, but at the same time had moved on. And there was something else, too: I felt no pressure. Well, I did. But it was all self-inflicted. As for external pressure? None. Everyone was all like, 'He's had seven months out of a car; he's never even driven these new ones. You can't expect him to be as good as he was.'

And despite that – or maybe even because of it – I found myself wondering, *Just a minute. How well could things go here?* After all, this was Monaco, a circuit I knew like the back of my hand, a mostly happy hunting ground over the 16 times I'd raced there. Yes, it was the scene of my worst accident (practice, 2003, a 185mph crash that earned me an overnight stay in hospital), but it was also the venue for one of my best-ever laps (2009, a qualifying lap for Brawn that put me on pole, from which I went on to win the race).

Added to all that, I used to live there, so it was virtually a home race for me.

So I started to dream. Not big. I'm no fool. It's not like I was thinking podium. But I hoped to finish in the top ten; I hoped to beat my teammate, Stoffel Vandoorne; and I hoped to be able to score the team's first points of the season.

Practice one came round and they started it up. I swallowed, riding the weirdest sensation that washed over me. A feeling of being like an alien in this car, that lasted as I dropped the clutch to pull out of the garage, going down the pit lane, watching the speed limiter and working out where all the buttons were on the steering wheel, all of which were so different from what I was used to.

I went out. The first corner is in the pit lane still, and then you go up the hill and then to Casino Square, by which time I just about had the hang of it. I remember going through Casino Square with the *biggest* smile on my face, because all of a sudden it felt so normal, so natural, and I was, like, *Are you kidding me? This is seven months off. It's a completely different car. And yet it all felt so normal to me. So brilliant.

By the end of the lap I felt full of renewed confidence that while things had moved on, they hadn't moved *that* far. It was still a car. It still had four wheels touching the road, and the steering wheel in my hands did what it always used to do.

Saturday. Qualifying. I was feeling good, and Q1 went well, in the sense that I was comfortably through into Q2 and feeling happy with the car. My confidence in it was growing and although I was still missing a bit on braking I was certain I could gain more.

What's more, I knew I'd left a bit out there on the circuit. In other words, there was still room for improvement.

My next lap didn't start too well. Bit of a braking SNAFU on turn one. But it didn't matter, because by the time I'd taken the little drag up the hill, it was ancient history and I was back to absolutely loving the drive, a huge grin stitched on my face as I eased it through Casino, getting the maximum out of it at last, touching the barrier a tiny bit on the way out, correcting a hint of oversteer. For the rest of what was a blissful lap I felt that I almost – almost – had the measure of the car.

'You're P9,' they told me at the end of it. 'You've qualified into Q3.'

Which was like pole position for me. I was on cloud nine.

What's more, I'd beaten Stoffel, my teammate, who had qualified tenth, and in Formula One the only real test of your individual strength as a driver is whether or not you can beat your teammate.

Two hours later I came back down to earth with a thump that must have registered on the Richter scale.

'We've got a problem.'

'What problem?'

'A problem with the engine. We're going to have to change it.'

'Meaning?'

'You'll have to start from the pit lane. So you're last.'

I was like, 'Did you know that this might happen?'

They cleared their throats and looked at their shoes. 'Yeah, we just didn't want to tell you before qualifying.'

I thought about it and climbed down from the ceiling, deciding that they'd probably done the right thing, because if I'd known about the possible engine problem then I probably wouldn't have performed so well and I'd have got nothing out of the weekend.

But yes, it hurt, especially as it was only my car, and Stoffel moved up to ninth as result, leaving me staring down the barrel of a Sunday race that was not going to be fun in the slightest.

And boy, was I right about that.

I woke up the next morning grimly contemplating a day of driving around Monaco for two hours being lapped – and nothing that anybody said could cheer me up.

Sure enough, as the race proceeded and a change of pit-stop strategy came to nothing, I sat there simmering, with Pascal Wehrlein in front of me – until, 50 laps into the 72-lap race, I could take it no more and spoke to my engineer. 'Can we just pit again, put new tyres on and then we'll see if we can catch and overtake Wehrlein?'

What did we have to lose? Monaco is terrible for overtakes – an average of 12 per race compared to 52 for somewhere like Shanghai. But that's still 12 overtakes, and there was no reason I couldn't be one of them.

Yes, they said. So I pitted, we put on another set of tyres and I set off again. The pace was good, especially when I was in clear air, and pretty soon I found myself going from being 20 seconds behind Wehrlein to catching him up – until I was right on his tail and thinking about making my move.

Again, what did I have to lose? If it worked it would be a great move. If it didn't, we'd crash, I'd hit the bar early and drink lots of beer.

It was just before the tunnel, the double right-hander. I came up alongside him on the inside. No one really overtakes there, but I was feeling pretty gung-ho and thought I'd have a go. To be fair, if he'd seen me, it would have been okay. It's just that…

He didn't.

And by the time I realised that he wasn't aware of me it was too late because he was already turning in, and we touched. *Ding*. As we did that, I braked, so my car went backwards, his shot forward, our tyres clashed – and that was enough to flip him over onto his side against the barrier.

Wehrlein had hurt his spine in a crash earlier that year, so I was worried about him. I couldn't see anything because the floor of his car was blocking my view, but I was close enough to know that his head was against the tyre wall. All I could do was pull away from his upturned car and make my way through the tunnel, creating more sparks than a welder on a deadline before pulling off the right-hand side at the other end.

As I got out of the car I heard that Wehrlein had clambered out of his Sauber unharmed, so at least he was okay. Probably cursing me, mind you. The accident was more my fault than his: 60/40, I'd say.

As for me, I had to do the walk of shame back to the paddock, the boats in the harbour on one side, the grandstands on the other, the crowd being kind enough to clap and wave as I trudged dejectedly past, even though they were probably thinking, *Look at him. What a wanker. He's just crashed when he was in last place.*

And still my day's woes were yet to end. Monaco is the only circuit where the paddock and the pit lane are in completely different places, and I reached the garages first. There I discovered that Stoffel had been running in tenth, and thus had been about to score the team's first point of the season. The mechanics had been levitating with excitement at the thought of scoring a point at last. But because of my little incident the safety car had gone out, which meant that all the cars had bunched up, and they were all on newer tyres than Stoffel, and so…

Well, in the end he hit the wall after being tipped off the track by Sergio Pérez, but I could tell they were pissed off at me. It was the little giveaways that did it. Like the way they looked at me, shook their heads and then threw their gloves on the floor.

I felt bad for them (while at the same time thinking, *For goodness sake, it's only a point. This is a team that should be fighting for the World Championship*) and left them to it, onto the second leg of my journey back to the paddock, interviews all the way down – can't say I was at my most gracious – until I got to the engineers. 'Sorry guys.'

'Don't worry,' they said, 'it happens. We shouldn't have put you in that position of starting last.' And then, when I saw the mechanics again after the race, they'd cooled down and I gave them all a hug and apologised, and they were, like, 'It's cool, it is what it is,' just that they were upset because that they'd lost a point, which would have been the first point of the season.

Except – what am I saying? As it turned out, I did in fact get two points out of that race.

I got two penalty points on my super licence for flipping Pascal Wehrlein against the tyre wall.

BEING A SELFISH BASTARD

(AND OTHER ESSENTIAL SKILLS)

My Monaco return wasn't a great day at the office, but there were upsides. Two upsides, in fact: first, I proved to myself that I could still drive bloody fast in an F1 car; second, the very act of going back became a way of checking whether I'd made the right decision to retire in the first place. After a boozy Sunday night I left on Monday morning with a hangover and the sure knowledge that I'd made the right call.

Yes, it had been nice to see the old faces again, but being back in the spotlight had reminded me how insular it was. How you never got off the plane and thought, 'Wow, this is someplace new', because the instant you arrived you were absorbed into the city that is Formulaoneville and it was the same city wherever you went in the world. Airport, hotel, circuit, back to the hotel, and that's it. You don't see anything else.

Wait. Don't get me wrong here. I'm talking about being a driver. As a spectator my love for the sport has never diminished, and if Monaco reaffirmed my decision to leave F1, it also reaffirmed my love of racing as a whole, something that's been in me since I was yea big. I won't go into the details of how I became a racing driver (there's another book for that), but mine was a path trodden by the likes of Ayrton Senna and Johnny Herbert; it took me through the ranks of junior karting and into Formula One, and it was a journey started by my father.

I'll be a dad myself by the time you read this and if my son, Hendrix Jonathan Button, wants to go racing then just you try and stop us. We'll be off for some important father–son bonding time: karting, probably, but not exclusively, because it's important to do all kinds of driving, not just the stuff that you like. You need to learn how to drive different vehicles, how they behave in varying conditions, how to brake, how to handle a circuit, how to slide, even going over jumps. It's all about building up general driving skill.

Me, I got my first go-kart when I was seven, mainly for something to do at the weekends because my parents had split up. My dad was great. He wasn't one of those tyrants I used to see shouting at their kids. I realise now the benefit of starting young. You're like a sponge, soaking up knowledge, learning at an age when it all goes in. But what's just as important is making sure it starts off being fun and stays that way, because if you're too focused and it becomes all-consuming then the chances are you'll hate it by the time you're 12.

I couldn't improve on the way that my dad it. He'd always say, 'If you're not enjoying it, or you want to take a break, tell me, and we'll stop.' We never did, of course.

TWELVE ESSENTIAL TOOLS
IN A DRIVER'S TOOLKIT

1. Natural skill

Ask me what is 'natural skill' and I'll look at you as though you're a bit hard of thinking and say something like, 'Well, it's skill, isn't it? Only skill that you already have,' and maybe I'll remember first getting into a kart all those years ago. How I just somehow *knew* what to do.

And I bet that every single driver on the grid of a Grand Prix had a similar experience, because the fact is that all drivers in Formula One have natural talent, just that some have more of it than others.

Lewis has oodles of it, for example. Put him in anything and he'll be quick. Then there are other drivers who have a natural gift but whose talent isn't quite as abundant as his and so have to work at it. Fernando Alonso is a good example, who has worked hard to improve his skills, working on any areas of weakness and to make certain that he can get the maximum out of the car and out of the team. If you ask me, Fernando is a good example of a complete driver because he understands how to supplement his natural ability with hard work.

And of course it's in your genes, somehow. Take a bow, Max Verstappen, whose father, Jos, was an F1 driver, and whose mother, Sophie Kumpen, was also a racing driver (she was my teammate in karting and she was so quick). Clearly, there's no doubt Max has inherited his parents' talent. Just look at the way that he can push a car in wet conditions. A great race for him was Brazil 2016, my second-to-last Grand Prix. It was wet but it was just unreal what Max could do with the car that most of the other drivers couldn't. I mean, he almost hit the wall and hurt himself badly, but he didn't. He kept it out there, and he had a great race. That's natural. That's not learnt.

For any driver, though, natural talent is not enough. Eventually, and providing that lady luck continues to smile on you with a full-faced idiot grin you'll be combining your God-given skill with experience, which is when you get to be a really deadly competitor, but you'll also need to be a grafter. A lot of drivers think they can skip that bit. A lot of drivers, especially when they first join the circus, will think being quick is enough.

Me, for example. Coming into Formula One in 2000 I believed my raw talent was enough. I was 20 years old, racing with Williams, a multiple World Championship winning team. That season I qualified third at Spa, which is one of the most difficult tracks in the world. I thought I was the mutt's nuts.

And then in 2001 the results stopped coming. Racing with Benetton, I was uncompetitive and outraced by my teammate, Giancarlo Fisichella, added to which I was maybe enjoying the trappings of wealth a bit too much.

I'll touch on this again later, but it was the team who brought me out of that dark place. They told me, 'You're quick, but you think it's easy. You think your driving skill is enough, but it's not.' They made me work harder, and after that I never stopped putting in the time and effort. I spent more time with the engineers than I did with my mates; more time in the garage than I did on yachts – and it paid off.

In brief: No matter how much talent you (think you) have, you need to supplement it with hard graft. Which brings me on to...

2. A burning desire to learn

Coming from karting to F1 was a big shock, because karting is the opposite of racing an F1 car. There's no power in a kart. Lots of grip, but no power. So it's just about being as smooth as possible. Some of that smoothness you carry across to Formula One – not being aggressive on the steering wheel, for example – but other things, like braking, you don't, because even though you've acquired race-craft and driving skills in karting, it's just a fraction of the learning needed to be at the top of your game in an F1 car – and if you can't adapt it could be the end of your career. If you come in and you're not quick enough or you make too many mistakes, you're out immediately. Remember Yuji Ide? Exactly.

Kevin Magnussen was my teammate in 2014. He'd won everything before he got to F1, and he thought he'd come into the sport, destroy his teammate (me) and be winning races. And he wasn't, of course, because he made the classic mistake that we all make of thinking that he was the finished article.

I remember him in the third race of the year saying to me, 'JB, I didn't realise how tough this was. How much I'd have to work.'

'Aha, Kevin,' I said, 'and that's because you're racing against the very best in the world, the crème de la crème – chaps who have so much experience, not just of racing, but also of setting up of a Formula One car. You should be learning as a racing driver, Kevin, especially when you get to a sport that's as complex as Formula One.'

I mean, maybe that's not an exact quote. But it was something just as articulate and wise as that.

In brief: It's important to have confidence in your ability, but also have the understanding that you need to learn, you should always be learning, you're never as good as you should be, you're never the greatest. In other words, never think you're the best – but strive to be.

3. The ability to be a selfish bastard

Sweeping statement alert: it's almost impossible to hold down a relationship and be a Formula One driver. It was Brittny, in the early days of our relationship, who pointed this out to me, probably as I was shouldering my bag and leaving to catch a flight. And while in the bad old days I might well have told her she was plain wrong, these days I'm old and ugly enough to realise that she was in fact totally on the money: I *was* very selfish, and, having bailed from F1, I'm a very different person now. I try to be kind and generous to a fault. And by the way, your hair really suits you like that.

Take Nico Rosberg, who won the World Championship in 2016 and then quit the sport. There were those who said that he'd bailed because he'd won the World Championship, that he was lucky and he knew Lewis would beat him next year.

I know there were those who said that, because I was one of them.

However, I've since heard him say something that resonated with me. He said, 'Sure, I could have gone on, trying to defend the title. But why? It's easy to want more, more, more, but you also have to be careful and not lose yourself as a person.'

I respect that and understand how he felt. Plus it was interesting to hear him say that, because not only had I never heard a driver say that before but because I've always felt like that myself: you have to forget about everything else in life and become a person that you might not like. You have to be very selfish.

There is, of course, a positive aspect to being selfish (having spent years at it I had to find something good) and it's the fact that you're focused on what you're doing, being in the right frame of mind, being as fit as possible, being ready for the start of the year. You also have to make sure that you get on well with the team and the sponsors, and though that sounds like the opposite of being selfish – quite nice of you, in fact – it's actually all about improving your standing and getting the best out of those around you so they'll work harder for you, and thus your competitiveness will improve. So, yeah, it's still pretty selfish.

In brief: In F1, everything is a selfish act until you stop being a driver, and then it's not.

4. A competitive nature

Am I competitive? Much more competitive than you, I bet.

And this is a terrible thing to admit, but I don't tend to compete at things that I can't win, which is one of the reasons I don't play any other sports. Here in LA I've taken up boxing and lifting weights, both things I'd never done and didn't want to do until Brittny badgered me into it. I love them both now, but only since I got good.

But I'm the same with anything. Like, if I do my shoelaces up and it takes longer than I think it should, that annoys me. Or, I don't know, measuring coffee beans for grinding and it's not 15 grams – or it is 15 grams, but I didn't do it as quickly as I did it the day before. Stuff like that. Stupid stuff.

And here's another sad thing to admit: if I hadn't been any good at racing I wouldn't have continued with it. I couldn't have stood people thinking, *You're not good enough*, and, worse, knowing it in my own heart. I'd have had to do something else – something else that channelled my competitive spirit.

In brief: If you're not super-competitive you're probably not cut out for sports. I mean: duh.

5. A team-player disposition

Despite Formula One's reputation for breeding prima donnas, there is in fact no room for them because F1 is a team sport, pure and simple.

Not that it was always the case, mind you, and it's taken teams and drivers a while to wake up to the fact that the most successful teams are the ones who work well together, which means that these days, drivers are spending more time at the factory. They've realised that they have to hang out with the engineers to understand the cars, because people who came before them have done it and achieved great things – drivers like myself and Fernando and Sebastian Vettel – drivers who put the time and effort in.

So now when a new driver comes in, the team says to them, 'You need to spend time with the engineer; you need to understand the car,' as well as spending a lot of time in simulators, which I never had when I was a kid. It was *Gran Turismo*, that was it. Or *Mario Kart*.

All this means that they're spending much more time understanding what the car can and can't do, they're a lot more prepared than they – by which I mean 'we' – used to be, and as a result they get into F1 cars and can be pretty quick straight away.

But there's a drawback. Kids who have spent a lot of time in simulators and not enough time on the track are in danger of suffering a huge setback when they crash. It knocks the stuffing out of them. A computer game helps you in many ways, but it doesn't help you understand how an impact feels, and we all have to crash one time in our lives to understand what G-force feels like – proper G-force, I'm talking 35G. It puts you in your place a little bit and you respect the car and the circuits a little bit more as a result.

We'll talk more about the simulator in a bit. The point being that young drivers are absorbed into a team-player culture quicker these days than ever before, and they understand that they're not driving for themselves, they're doing it for the team.

So when, for example, you crash the car, you're devastated. Not for yourself, you don't give a shit about yourself, but for the mechanics, all those guys who have worked flat out to build the car, who've now got to stay up all night – because they do, you know – and do it all again.

They're the guys for whom you reserve your sympathy and your apologies; they're the first people you see when you come in after you've stacked the car up against the wall. Not the team boss. You'll speak to him or her last. You walk around every single mechanic and you say sorry. Most of the time the mechanics will pat you on the back and say, 'Shit happens, mate, it's great that you were pushing,' And then and only then will you speak to the team boss. But that bit doesn't matter so much; you don't mind about that, that's just a 'sorry for crashing your car', which he should be all right about, because for him it's just a case of finding money in the budget, which – this being Formula One – he should be able to do with comparative ease.

After that you might even spend time in the garage with the mechanics when they're rebuilding. If you see drivers rolling their sleeves up and getting busy with a wrench then it's probably just for TV: the moment the cameras leave the mechanics are snatching the tools out of the driver's hand and shooing them off to a safe distance before they can do any damage. Even so, the mechanics like drivers to be there. They want you to see and appreciate the amount of work that's going into this extraordinary piece of kit.

Even when they're not working on the car, it's worth spending a bit of time with them. You'll never be a fully paid-up member of their gang – mechanics are a breed unto themselves, the garage a closed society – but you can learn from them and they can learn from you. Day to day they'll hear you shouting at your engineer but they rarely hear first-hand what you have to say about the car or what you think about the team, and I think they deserve to hear it.

I'd often go out for a booze-up with my engineers and mechanics post-race. They'd have a few beers, say what they really thought, and sometimes it wasn't especially flattering. 'I thought you were a bit of a dick at such-and-such a time.' And more often than not they'd be right about that.

But then you crash the car one morning at practice, you need it ready for qualifying and it's touch and go if they can get it ready in time. Maybe if you're the guy who's been out boozing with them, accepted the piss-take and admitted you were a dick then they'll go that extra mile to get it done for qualifying. But if you're not that person, and you're not showing them love and letting them know how important they are to the team, then maybe they won't have that extra 10 per cent in caring whether the car's built for qualifying or not; maybe they'd be, like, 'Oh, sorry, mate, it wasn't quite ready.'

So there's that. There's also the fact that as the driver you're a kind of link between the garage, the engineers, management and the sponsors, and by the simple expedient of stopping off in the garage to wish everyone a good night you can help with that all-important sense of belonging and communal effort otherwise known as team spirit.

And there's the fact that ultimately everything you do is for the selfish reason that you want to be quicker come the race, and the more people you have on your side the more likely that is to happen (ahem, see number three).

In brief: Go out for beers with your mechanic and engineers, get your round in and they'll soon open up; they'll tell you if and when you're behaving like a dick and you'll thank them for it later.

6. The ability to work well with sponsors

It's Silverstone, Grand Prix weekend, and I'm stepping into a helicopter, interrupting what should be a weekend of laser-sharp racing focus in order to fly to a sponsor meeting. I've got my best ingratiating smile in my top pocket and I'm ready to go.

Crucially, the McLaren marketing department haven't told me what the meeting is about, and I haven't asked because it isn't that important to me what the meeting is about. The key thing is that I know what is required, which is to represent McLaren.

I was a bit of sponsor-meeting monster when I was at McLaren. A sponsor-friendly driver has a lot to do with whether a sponsor stays at a team or goes and, thankfully, I was one of the most sponsor-friendly drivers in the paddock. It was one of the reasons they kept me on as a representative after my retirement. I remember it being an absolute wake-up call. *Wait. So I'm in control of whether the sponsors stay or go? Mwah-ha-ha..*

Truth is, though, I enjoyed that part of the job and I knew that more often than not, I nailed it. I see kids coming into the sport now and they haven't got a Scooby what to do in front of the sponsors. These are companies putting £50 million into a team. It's a massive deal. And drivers just stand there staring out from under the peaks of their snapbacks and gawping like guppy fish.

So anyway. Silverstone. They fly me from Silverstone for this meeting, we walk in and it's Deutsche Bank.

I say to marketing, 'Er, can I have a word?'

We go outside. I say, 'You do know that I'm an ambassador for Santander and I have been for five years. I know you know this because you sorted the deal.'

'Yes,' says the marketing bod, 'but this is fine. This is for the future.'

I say, 'I'm still contracted, I've got another year.'

He's, like, 'Oh, it'll be fine.'

At this point, I have to do what the team say. So I'm sitting in a meeting about a bank sponsor for the team when I'm sponsored by a rival bank, which is awkward to say the least.

But of course I wear my ingratiating smile and play my part, which is to convey that whether we win or lose, we at McLaren work hard, and that we're a great family that you, the sponsor, absolutely want to be a part of.

And that's my job because as I say, I'm like a hub in the team. The bosses know many things about the future of the team, but in terms of where the car is – its performance and future direction – that's something that only the engineers, mechanics and the driver know, and like it or not, the sponsors don't want to talk to the engineers and mechanics. They want to talk to the driver.

The drivers are the personalities who represent the team and therefore they become the public faces of any brand that aligns itself to the team. So if the sponsor doesn't like the driver, it's an uphill battle for the team to make a deal.

So it's a strange situation, but I actually quite enjoyed it, knowing that what I said and did actually made a difference to whether we succeeded or not.

More on sponsors later, but for the time being…

In brief: If you think you're just a racing driver and not a salesman as well, think again.

7. Fitness

More on fitness to come. For the time being I just want to leave this here.

8. Luck

You know how people say you make your own luck? That's bollocks. If a car spins off the circuit in front of you and you beat it, that's not you 'making your own luck', that's just luck. He spun off the circuit and you benefited because he's been unfortunate or made a mistake.

Racing at Suzuka in May, 2019, I was in sixth place at the weekend and the Mugen NSX in front of me got a puncture, pulled out and I went up to fifth. That was good luck. Later on, I got a puncture myself. That was bad luck.

In brief: Luck is swings and roundabouts. Sometimes we get it, sometimes we don't. Be sure to make the best of it when you do. That's all I have to say about that.

9. Self-belief

What's the difference between arrogance and self-belief?' I think self-belief is believing in yourself. Arrogance, on the other hand, that's when you're shouting it from the rooftops. Ask someone with self-belief if they're the best in the world and they'll give you a little wink or the smile that says, "What do you think I think?" Ask an arrogant bleeder if he's the best in the world and he'll be shouting it from the rooftops. So that's the big difference. They know they are, but they don't shout it out.

In brief: Acquiring self-belief is a whole other thing, of course. For that you need…

10. Support

When you start your career, you think that everyone you meet is looking out for you. You believe that everyone is a well-wisher, every pat on the back a purely selfless act.

It's a common tale in sports and entertainment: somebody makes various promises, and because you're young (for which read naïve) and you're walking around with a big Snoopy grin on your face because you can't believe your luck, and because the money's coming in, you don't really do much questioning.

Then one day the penny drops that you haven't got quite as much as you should and your gaze turns to the guy in the corner puffing on a big cigar and sitting on a big pile of money.

After that, you go the opposite way. You suddenly become ultra-suspicious, you only trust those in your inner circle, which means you go through a period of suspecting people's motives. You think, *Why does this person want to be my mate?* Is it because they like me as a person? Or do they *want* something?

That's the situation I was in for, oh, about 13 of the 17 years I was in the sport. It was only latterly that I really started to open up. If I got into a relationship and discovered they weren't really interested in me as a person I could deal with it, whereas when I was younger I couldn't.

Living in LA you have to be careful. People there are always looking for an angle, but I'm willing to let them in and see where it takes us as friends. I'm a lot more open to that; I'm much stronger and I can handle it if it all goes tits up.

As for that inner circle, mine has been incredible. First off, there was my dad. There was never any doubt that he had my best interests at heart. When it came to racing, everything he said and did was for me. He never had a hidden agenda.

Having said that, I didn't take on board everything he told me. I used him to bounce ideas off, but if I didn't like his response I would often snap at him. If his answer or his reasoning wasn't what I wanted to hear, I let him know about it. For example, he'd be saying, 'I think you need to spend more time with the mechanics, make them feel part of the team, you know,' something like that.

I'd be like, 'Dad, come on, I'm doing enough.'

But then I'd think about it and realise he was right. Years later, I'd even be including it as a piece of essential advice in this very book. And the reason he was right was that he saw things from another angle; he stood back in the garage, saw the guys at work, noted how I interacted with them and thought there was room for improvement. It's one of the few things I regret in life, snapping at Papa Smurf.

But at least I can say that I came round. And I can say when it happened, too, because it was in 2009, my Championship-winning year. The season began spectacularly well for me – I won six of the first seven races – after which things were, shall we say, a little more trying. And that's when it really hit home to me that I couldn't do this on my own. Before that year I'd always felt that I was getting the best out of the car. No one ever thought we had a race-winning car, so there wasn't that pressure; I could just go out and enjoy my racing. It was a little bit frustrating that we weren't winning races, but we were fighting for podiums and it was great, it was fun, every success was a bonus that exceeded all of the expectations placed upon me.

Then suddenly we had a chance to fight for the Championship and wouldn't you just know it but the pressure from the team and the outside world increased exponentially.

History tells us that I was doing phenomenally well at the beginning of the season – until suddenly I wasn't. My teammate, Rubens Barrichello, was doing a better job in certain races and I felt the Championship was maybe slipping from my grasp.

More pressure. In an interview somebody asked me, 'Do you not want to win this Championship?' and I responded sarcastically. It was a dumb, unprofessional thing to do (despite the fact that it *was* a stupid question, and I saw other journalists shaking their heads at just how stupid it was), but it became a bit of a watershed moment nonetheless, the point at which I thought, *Hang on, no, I can't do this on my own, I need support.*

And, sure, when you're down, and the pressure's on, that's when you cast about looking for other opinions.

It shouldn't have taken being down for me to do that, but it did, and I'm glad it happened because at least I finally opened myself up to the advice of others. Not for the purpose of blowing smoke up my arse and telling me how good I was, but to remind me of what I'd achieved at the start of that season, making me feel comfortable with having a bad race, because we all have bad races, and it's all about learning from them and coming back stronger.

I remember my dad saying to me that year, 'Is it okay for me to say how I feel?' and I was, like, 'Yes, I promise you I won't be snappy, I want to hear what you've got to say,' and that was a real turning point in my career. I began listening to the people around me and using their support, understanding that they were being helpful in my time of need. I realised how much they meant to me.

The fact is that whether you take it with a pinch of salt or take it seriously, you've got to listen to others' opinions, because they see things that you don't. I wish it hadn't taken adversity to make me realise that, because I know now that you can always be better as a person and as a driver through listening – because that's how you learn.

Mikey was a really calming influence, because the only time I got to relax was when I was getting a massage over a race weekend, when he'd talk me through the race. 'What do you want from this weekend? What would you be happy with? Where do you think you need to improve?'

I don't even know if he was listening to my answers – probably not – but it was great to have that sounding board. As Brits, we're not very good at talking about our feelings, most of us anyway, so you need people around you who can draw that out of you. Having read a bunch of books by the life coach Tony Robbins I've begun to wish I'd had someone like that in F1, someone to whom you can talk who doesn't have a vested interest in you.

On the other hand, I would have never wanted my teammate or a rival from another team knowing I was seeing a therapist. However you're feeling on the inside you've got to look strong and confident. There's no room for doubt in motorsport, because in motorsport if you doubt yourself, other people will doubt you as well. Big shout out, then, to those I've already mentioned – Richard, Mikey, Chrissy, James – as well as my PA, Jules Gough – all of whom were there for the bad times as well as the good, and are still with me.

In brief: It's not just a case of remembering that you need support, it's about listening to that support and letting that support know that their contribution is welcome and valued.

11. The right mental attitude

In LA I go karting with a bunch of kids who beat me every time. Does it bother me? No.

Well, okay, it does bother me a bit. Quite a lot, actually. But it's not as though I have a problem with it. It's not like I'm throwing my crash helmet at the fence and decking stewards in my anger. That's because, firstly, I'm not in the habit of chucking helmets and decking stewards at the best of times; and secondly, I'm not afraid to lose.

It's true. Despite everything I've already said about having a competitive nature, I really don't mind losing. I *care*. Oh yes. And I plan to get better the next time I'm sitting behind the wheel. But it doesn't scare me, and that's the crucial difference.

Plus – and here's the important bit – I know I can improve. I mean, I'll always get quicker. Even at 39, I reckon I could spend two weeks in a kart and be good enough to race. Probably wouldn't win, but I would race competitively.

It's the same for me and GT racing. I've had to put the time and effort in and not get frustrated when it wasn't plain sailing. An F1 car is open-wheeled. It's single-seater. It's all about the aerodynamics. A GT car is none of the above. Pretty much all they have in common is four wheels. Even the steering wheel's a different shape.

So there's still so much left to learn before I hang up my cap for good. My ultimate aim is to be that 'complete driver' I'm talking about, and maybe even go one better than the likes of Fernando. After all, the categories he's chosen have high down-force. He's not racing anything like Super GT or rallying, and that's when it gets more difficult, which is when you really learn. So that's what I'm looking forward to over the next few years. I'm looking forward to doing more learning.

I remember speaking to Alain Prost – one of my childhood heroes – because I was interested in getting a team together for rallycross, which is rally but around a circuit, banging wheels and everything. It's great fun. 'Would you be interested in being my teammate, Alain?' I asked him.

That would be so cool. Alain Prost as my teammate.

'Only do it if I could test every day.'

Cue the sound of fizzling fireworks.

'What?' I said.

With typical Gallic insouciance he said, 'I would never get in a car and race if I'm not up there with the best of them.'

He wanted to test for weeks before we went racing and most teams don't have the budget for that. Now, as it happens, the team didn't get off the ground anyway, but the fact is most teams don't have the budget for that kind of testing, so Alain was counting himself out.

At the time I was disappointed, but I totally got where he was coming from. He knew what we all know, that it takes time. You can't just jump in anything and be the quickest; there will always be drivers in every category who are experts at what they do, who will be very, very difficult to beat.

Put simply, if you have too much ego you'll never succeed in other forms of motorsport, because you'll arrive, you won't be much cop, and you'll reach the conclusion that the equipment is at fault, when the blame lies with you.

Equally, you will never be a good driver if you don't eat, sleep and breathe F1. There's no such thing as a brilliant driver with a passing interest in the sport. When I was racing in F1, I didn't think about anything else apart from racing in F1. So on a Sunday night after the race, whether it was good or bad, I'd want to get straight back in the car. Pretty much, the whole time I was not racing, I wanted to be in the car.

As you might imagine, I struggled to relax. Whether I was driving the car or not, it was all Formula One: how can I be better as a driver? How can I put right the mistakes I made the weekend before, or, if I had won the race, how could I do an even better job? As a result, I was so drained at the end of the season, I'd get ill. You never fall ill during the season, always at the end.

Is it a strength or a weakness, that inability to switch off? You might argue that the ability to focus is a good one, but on balance I'm marking it down in the minus column. If I'd had a negative race, that negativity would stay with me and I was very bad at being able to put it behind me, at which point it started to have a slightly poisoning effect.

I think that's why racing took such a toll on me over 17 years, and why it was so tough for me, mentally and physically. Why I retired. I couldn't deal with it any more.

In brief: Don't be afraid to lose and try – if you can (and if you can then you're a stronger person than I am) – not to let it take over your life.

12. A strong nerve (but not outright fearlessness)

Crashing is inevitable. The trick is to come out the other side. Some of the reason why you can carry on after a big shunt is because you've survived and you look at yourself, and you think, *I hit that wall at 140 miles an hour and I'm still here. How is that possible?* Because in a road car, you'd be dead; you'd be a millimetre thick, whereas in an F1 car you're surrounded by goodness: you've the carbon-fibre tub, the spongey headrest; you're wearing a carbon-fibre helmet and you've got the HANS device, which stops your head from going too far forward and breaking your neck.

Then you've got the circuits, which are built for safety. It's not like it used to be with a bunch of tyres stacked on top of each other. Now they're proper safety barriers.

So you're in a car that's safe, on a circuit that's safe, surrounded by state-of-the-art apparatus whose sole function is to keep you safe. But even so, you don't want to crash, and not just because it's expensive and embarrassing and messes up your team's weekend. Firstly because, well, you know, there's always the possibility that something bad will happen, that something will go wrong and that those safety features will fail you or be insufficient. Because crashing is scary shit.

Secondly, because fearlessness can make you a poor driver. You're never going to finish a race if you're a fearless – for which read 'reckless' – driver. 'Mad' Max Verstappen, for example, has gone through his period of being fearless, crashed a lot, learnt to exercise caution and come out the other side a better driver because of it. Think about Niki Lauda, who in 1976 showed unbelievable courage to return to racing just three races after the fiery accident that almost claimed his life. Reaching the last race of the season in Japan it was raining, horrific weather, and Lauda withdrew, refusing to race and in doing so handing the World Championship to James Hunt. Even someone as fearless as him understood the danger, and knew when to step back and say, 'I'm not a superhero.'

In brief: There's a difference between being brave and being fool-hardy, and a lot of it comes down to age and experience.

THE TOO-LONG-DIDN'T-READ VERSION

- Love your racing
- Love to learn
- Keep yourself in physical and mental shape
- Don't be a dick.

DRIVING LIKE A PRO

EVEN WHEN YOU'RE A BEGINNER

Something I've realised: we're not F1 drivers, we're racing drivers. We love racing things. And the advantage of leaving F1 is that I have the freedom to drive other things, and that is properly awesome.

Is it a speed thing? A boys' toys thing? No. Don't think so. I flew a Learjet once; the pilot let me have a go while I was renting it. The weird thing is, you turn and if you don't pull back, the nose dips. Also when you're turning, you're turning from the rear, so you have oversteer the whole time, which I hate – I hate oversteer – so I was turning and the rear was turning, not the front, and it was the weirdest feeling. Ugh.

I've also flown a propeller plane. I even lined it up for the runway at Guernsey, which was pretty awesome, especially as Guernsey was the intended destination. Generously, I let the pilot take the controls when we got too low.

Other than that, no, I don't have the urge to race planes, or boats. As far as I'm concerned, you've got to have tyres on the road. And four of them at that. I drove a three-wheeler car once and didn't get on with it, because I just didn't get the right feeling from it. I drive with my bum a lot more than with my feet or hands. I *feel* the car with my arse, and I need two tyres on the road at the back to do that.

All of which is a roundabout way of saying that even though I've left F1 – at least as a driver – I very much have *not* left racing. For a start, I've been doing a lot of karting here in LA. Will I ever be as good as I was when I was 17? No, is the answer. But I can have a laugh trying, and it's great fun to mess with people's expectations. After all, I'm an old geezer (I'm not really an old geezer, I'm 39, but in karting terms I'm ancient) and people don't expect me to be quick in a kart because I'm from Formula One and the two worlds are so far apart. You don't expect the winner of Wimbledon to be ace at ping-pong just because they both involve a ball, a net and the potential for a backhand smash.

The bigger question for me is whether I'd really want to aim that high. To which the answer, again, is probably no. I just want to continue enjoying it and the best way for me to stop enjoying something is to start putting myself under pressure. What's the point of escaping the intense environment of F1 just to be in another pressure cooker?

So no, I'd like to do some club races here in America. It'll be cool, turning up in a transit van to karting – just like the old days with Dad. I'm even getting my old Rocket colour scheme sorted for the Karts.

Mainly, though, my actual racing job these days is Super GT.

I've dropped the G-bomb a few times. 'GT'. And if you've been wondering what it's all about, read on, because in my opinion, GT Racing is the best in the world. And I'm not just saying that because in 2019 I won the Super GT Championships with my Japanese team, Team Kunimitsu. Or maybe I am. I dunno. I'll have to give that one a bit more thought.

Not to be confused with GT3, which is basically the super-cars that you see on the road stripped out, strengthened, and with a roll cage put in, a Super GT car has a carbon-fibre monocoque, like a Formula One car, but is big enough for two people, with a shell that sits on top of it. This thing has 650 horsepower, lots of downforce – not as much as in an F1 car, but still a lot – and they weigh about 1,000kg, 350kg more than an F1 car, which from a driving point of view may well be the biggest difference between the two, and is definitely what makes them about 15 seconds a lap slower than an F1 car. Racing only in Japan, at Suzuka, which just happens to be my second-favour-ite-ever circuit, and the old F1 track in Fuji, it's called Super GT, because it's… um, super.

I first drove one in 2016 when I was still racing in F1. Honda, who were supplying engines for McLaren, have a Honda Thanks Day every year, where fans can see the cars driving around in Motegi: F1 cars, Indy cars, Super GT, loads of different motorbikes. I used the opportunity to bag myself a test on the Super GT car, had so much fun in it and said to the guys, 'Is there any possibility of me racing that car in 2018?'

And they said, 'We'd love you to race! Why don't you do the Suzuka 1000K?'

This was a one-off race that I ended up driving in 2017 (the only two races I did in 2017 were the Monaco GP in F1 and that) with the Mugen Motorsports team. So I drove for them and had a great time. I mean, it wasn't a good race, we had a couple of punctures and a drive-through penalty, so we didn't finish very high up but, I had a blast doing it, so when they said, 'Do you want to do 2018?' I was like, *Bring it on.*

Honda has five cars in the Super GT all run by different teams, but there was one team in particular that I wanted to drive for, Team Kunimitsu, because I'd watched them for years, appreciated their history and admired their driver, Naoki Yamamoto, who is now my teammate.

It's a challenge. Though there is downforce in Super GT it's more mechanical-grip driven, and because I'm an aerodynamic guy, and I've spent years honing my skills of working with aerodynamics and not mechanical grip, which is tyres and suspension, I'm still not there. It's a very different way of driving. But I like a challenge. I like to learn.

All of the debriefs are in Japanese, and my Japanese pretty much stops and starts at 'sushi' and 'sake'. And since there's very little raw fish talk in a racing debrief, I just stand there like a lemon waiting for them to finish so we can try and speak English together.

I must admit, I thought I'd arrive in Japan, enjoy the great racing then get out of the car and be chilled enough to let them do the work. But no, it turns out that I can't quite switch off. I want to be involved. I want to help make the car quicker, which can be difficult when you're English speaking and, the inexperienced one in the team. All the time when we test, it's my teammate they test first. He's the number one, which is so surreal and not something I've ever had in in Formula One before, where it's virtually unheard of for teams to play favourites (despite the suspicions and accusations that constantly arise)

It's a slightly hermetic life, different from what I was used to in Formula One. Not only are there are eight races a year and I travel to Japan probably another eight or nine times for testing as well – which is a whole heap of long-haul flights – but there's a lot of waiting around, and I spend plenty of time sitting around looking at my phone and eating cold bento boxes. Some days I get to the circuit at 9.30am and don't strap into the car until 2.30pm.

What makes it worthwhile is the racing, which is properly awesome. Naoki and I won the Championship in 2018 and there was great fighting over each of the eight races, right to the very end of the season. It was brilliant, especially when you consider that it was my debut season.

At the time of writing, I'm still racing, but we'll have to see what happens in 2020. What I would love to do in the future

– and it might be as early as next year – is race in America. NASCAR would be great and, as you'll soon discover, I've got plans to do something with off-road trucks, although that's more for shits and giggles.

As for paid-for racing, I feel that my future will definitely be going down the aero route, which would be racing IMSA in America. IMSA cars are similar to Le Mans cars: 650 horse-power, completely carbon monocoque – like a Formula One car but with a roof and flip-up doors. With the engineering being closer to what I've been used to working with in Europe, I know that getting into that car, I'd be competitive – perhaps even more competitive than I have been in Super GT – chiefly because it's downforce-driven. Taking part you've got ex-F1 drivers, ex-Indy car drivers, former drivers from other categories doing it, which is great. There are some real characters in that game. To cap it all off they have the centrepiece race, the Daytona 24 Hours, which is the big one. You get a Rolex if you win, which would really impress my missus.

In the meantime, I have a team in GT3 – it's a full-on name, Jenson Team Rocket RJN – which races in Europe. Non-profit so far, and it doesn't take up masses of my time, but I love the fact that we're bringing the Rocket name back, which was my father's karting name, and I'd love to help some young talent through the GT ranks. Maybe even my own son, eventually.

What else? Well, endurance races are great because they're such a team effort. Even without the best car, you can still win simply by doing a better job as a team. But, for me, it would be a Championship thing, I prefer to compete in Championships, because it's only over a whole season that you really know whether or not you've done a better job than the other guys. When you win a race the emotions are very high; your adrenalin's through the roof. Team Kunimitsu won a race last year and the guys were crying their eyes out, but we won the Championship and they were much more reserved. It's more that little wink, like, *We did it*. It's that feeling that lives with you forever. You're a Champion, you haven't *been* a Champion, you *are* a Champion. I know that from my World Championship in Formula One. It's never going to go away. It's with me forever.

HOW NOT TO BUY A YACHT

(AND OTHER LIFESTYLE CHOICES)

Your flights are booked, your hotel reservation is sorted and you're given a schedule that you don't really need to consult because you have other people to do that for you. Everything, in short, is sorted so that you can focus on the job at hand, which is to drive a car really, really fast around a circuit. Unless you're doing a sponsor event, of course, in which case your job is to be picked up, hang around for about half an hour, do some pictures and then more often than not be taken out to dinner to a restaurant of your choosing. And, to cap it all off, on top of that you've got…

1. THE BOOZE-UPS

Older Formula One drivers have it all their own way. They can do shit and get away with it. Like if they're pictured drinking with their mates in St-Tropez, it's fine. It's them letting off steam. Go them!

It's the youngsters who don't have it so easy. The ones coming into the game. For them it's all, 'Oh, look at that playboy, who does he think he is? It's all gone to his head.' Basically, if you want to avoid the wagging fingers and the pointing tongues then you've got to be really careful as a youngster coming through the ranks.

Guess who wasn't careful?

And yes, people ask if it went to my head. Actually they just straight out tell me, 'it went to your head, JB', as though they can presume to know what was going on inside my brains. But the people who say that can take a long walk off a short pier, because I don't think it did go to my head. Not really. What they interpreted as arrogance was in fact the euphoria of someone who was simply happy to be living his dream. How happy? Like a dog with two tails.

I know now that I didn't focus as much as I should have done. I didn't study and learn the engineering side of things. I didn't knuckle down and think, *This is just the start, but now I need to be clever and I need to work hard.* Like I say, I know that now, with the benefit of these hindsight goggles I'm currently wearing.

But at the time? Come on. I was a Formula One driver, I was racing for Williams. I was 20 years old, which at the time made me the youngest-ever F1 driver, and I thought my talent was all I needed to get by. So what was I going to do? I was going to go out.

So I did. And for a while, I stayed out. I mean, look, I come from Somerset where the local nightclubs were proper sticky-floor pick-up joints. Now suddenly I'm racing in Formula One and London has opened its doors and ushered me inside. I'm no longer at Oscars at Longleat or McGuinness's in Frome. I'm at China White in the West End, Mahiki in Mayfair, the Atlantic and the Titanic. I hadn't made new friends when I started in Formula One; I was still hanging out with my old mates from home, and together we were on the same fun, exciting journey, running around London trying to outwit the paparazzi because we needed to keep it all secret from my dad, who would have had a fit if he'd known I was living it up so much.

Having said all that, it wasn't nearly as debauched as your dirty mind is imagining, and while I might not have been *quite* as committed as I should have been, I was still a sportsman and very much aware of my responsibilities. Sure, I was out a lot, but I didn't let it get in the way of races. In terms of cutting things fine, probably the naughtiest thing I did was that I once partied on a Wednesday before a British Grand Prix. Oh yes, and I attended a *Scream* premier once, went on to the after-party and woke up a bit hung over. That was really the closest I ever got to drinking before a Grand Prix weekend.

After the races. Ah, now that's a different story. That was when the drinking would happen. Rapunzel had nothing on us when it came to letting our hair down. I remember after a Silverstone I partied for five days non-stop, out every night, and one of those nights consisted of me leaving the property where I was staying, wearing only Ugg boots and running around the block, which was much bigger than expected. The *block* was much bigger than expected, I should clarify.

Of course, the golden rule is that it's okay to do all this sort of stuff when things are on the up, but it's not a good look when results aren't going your way. Suddenly it's, 'Uh oh, so that's why he's no longer competitive. It's because he's out on the town every night'. That was what happened to me during my time at Benetton in 2001. True, the car wasn't up to much, but that's not really the barometer of your success as a driver. For that you need to look at how you perform against your teammate, who's driving exactly the same car as you, and I was getting soundly beaten by mine, Giancarlo Fisichella. I was in a slump. I was getting flak, not only from the press but also from my own boss, Flavio Briatore, who had called me 'a lazy playboy' (not true – I was a highly committed and industrious playboy).

Anyway. Like I say, the team had a word, put me straight. And during the off-season I switched up, got my shit together and focused on the engineering side of things. And after that the results started to come. Funny that.

My change of approach didn't stop me partying completely, of course. It just gave my work–social life the same thing I look for in my cars: balance. I'd still be up for it on Sunday night, post-race when we'd be like, 'Where's the party?' Me, Daniel Ricciardo, David Coulthard, anyone else we could rope in.

You do a bit of party-hopping, of course. *This one's good, but let's try this one. Oh, it's not quite as good, let's go back to the first one, oh no, we should have stayed at this one all along,* but we'd normally find out where the best parties were, and we'd do our best to play catch-up with the rest of our teams, many of whom would have been partying every night of the weekend – especially at Monaco, which is just huge for the teams, the fans, the visiting VIPs – everybody's on it all weekend, apart from the drivers. (Was I jealous, after my night on the Evian, seeing them all with their hangovers? Not a bit of it, mate. They'd all be going, 'Oh, we had a great night last night, so much fun,' and I'd be thinking, *Awesome, but I get to drive an F1 car today and that's pretty damn cool as well.*)

Besides, Sunday after Monaco was – probably still is – a blast. If you go to Amber Lounge it's, like, €600 a ticket just to get in and then you've got to pay for your drinks and for a table. You're talking €6,000 and the night's hardly even started. If you're a punter. It's different for drivers, of course. Everybody wants the drivers there because it attracts money, knowing that the drivers are in the party. And once you're there you don't get bothered. You have a VIP drivers' area, and the security guy follows you to the toilet to make sure everything's okay (which it would be, except for the fact that you have security guys following you to the toilet).

After winning Monaco in 2009, things got seriously messy. We partied after the race and then the next day, Monday, as the principality began to get back to normal after the weekend's festivities, we started drinking again, about midday this was. Sitting at a bar on the beach, we were downing bottles of rosé, texting people to join us until there was a whole crew, and between the lot of us we caned ten magnums of rosé.

Next the call went up for a club, which opened especially for us, and there they opened a huge bottle of champagne, a balthazar, that is in fact 16 normal bottles of champagne in one (dwarfing my winner's jeroboam, which is four bottles in one) and then we drank that, and then, just as we were winding down about to leave, they cracked open another one.

In the end, we finished at about one in the morning, and the next day christened our 13 hours of drinking 'Super Monday', which went on to became a bit of a Monaco tradition, podium or not.

Meanwhile, things have changed a bit. Back then there was a right crew – Michael Schumacher and David Coulthard to name but two – who all used to party after the race. Now it feels a little different. And while there are still some drivers painting the town various shades of red on a regular basis – don't worry, I won't tell your mum, Max – they're the exception rather than the rule. A lot of them go home. It's a very different atmosphere. We were like, *Do your job, let off steam*; they're like, *Do your job, go home*. I wonder if it's social media, your every move photo-graphed, tweeted and tracked, which we didn't have 20 years ago, thank God.

As for me, I prefer restaurants these days. Parties? Nah. Night-clubs? Definitely not. Give me a good restaurant any day. Besides I can't deal with the hangovers.

2. THE MONEY

Let's talk about the wages. According to the 2019 *Forbes* list, Lewis is F1's top earner with $55m in earnings and $10m in endorsements on top of that. Sebastian is behind him with $40.3m in earnings and $0.3m in endorsements, although both of them are some way behind the leader, some bloke called Lionel Messi, whose combined earnings is $127m.

(Who, though, is the highest-paid sportsman *of all time*? Answer at the end of the chapter.)

How Lewis and Sebastian's cumulative earnings would stack up, I couldn't say. Lewis is a five-time World Champion, Sebastian is *only* a four times World Champion. But Sebastian has been earning for longer. He won multiple World Championships at Red Bull and then he went to Ferrari for which he would have been paid a big lump sum.

So that's what you've got at the top end. But it's not the case right the way through the grid, because at the bottom end there are probably six or more drivers in F1 who don't get paid and instead have to bring money to the sport in order to compete. They will be paid through the sponsorship money they can generate.

I'm not going to talk about my earnings. Suffice to say that when I arrived in F1, I was paid half-a-million dollars in my first year, and to say I was happy with that as a 20-year old from Somerset is the understatement of the millennium. The fact that it was my starting salary, and that, all being well, things were only going get better from there was exciting. It's a huge, huge step-up, a real through-the-looking-glass moment, and it's sobering (metaphorically, not literally); it increases your sense of responsibility, your sense of social guilt, you name it.

Most of all it's brilliant. Not just because of the amount, but also because you're being paid so much for something you'd happily do for free. I swear to God that nobody comes into Formula One in the pursuit of fame and fortune. They might get it once they're there, but that's not the reason anyone embarks on this as a career. They do it because they love racing. And so when you're one of the lucky few who reaches the top and you're racing at the very pinnacle of the sport, and you're being paid that much money for it – it's just unreal.

Like I say, my earnings increased. They peaked in 2006, 2007, 2008 – the Honda years – and then dipped at Brawn, when the team said, 'We can't pay you what your contract says,' to which I replied, 'Okay, but I want to go racing, and I think this car could be good, so I'll take a pay cut.'

So it's big money, any way you look at it. And that's before you factor in the bonuses. Some drivers will earn a $1m bonus if they win a race. Just one race. The funny thing, though, is that you don't normally get a bonus for winning a Driver's Championship. It's the Constructor's Championship that's worth the big bucks because that's when the team gets the large payout – €100 million or something – from the FIA, and you can buy a lot of team-branded polo shirts with that.

It's the same as it is in football, where players are paid more than the people who manage them, the inverse of just about every other situation in life. Someone like Lewis is not only the highest paid person in the team, but also probably the highest paid person in the whole of Daimler AG, Mercedes' parent company. Even the CEO isn't going to be on the kind of money Lewis gets paid.

Still, you have to remember that the earning window is much smaller: for the first few years you have to prove yourself, after which you probably have ten years of earning good money and you could maybe push it for a few more years after that. And then? Well, you better find some other way of earning a crust.

In my own case, having left McLaren in 2016, I could have gone to other teams and earned reasonable money, but it wasn't about that; it was time to move away from the sport. Plus I knew that after F1, I could still earn money doing *something*. I just hadn't yet figured out what.

3. THE GLAMOUR

When I watch Formula One, I watch the racing. But you'd need a heart of stone – or be Kimi Räikkönen – not to feel a little excitement at all the glamour and glitz of the whole thing. Of course you love the driving. We're all there for that. But there's all the other stuff that goes with it. It's always in the back of your mind. I probably haven't really considered it before, but as a kid the glamour of F1 must have attracted me on some level, because otherwise why aim for that, rather than another class of racing? I'll have to get back to you on that one.

It's a particularly international sort of glamour, of course. Premiership footballers have the fast cars and the top clobber, but so do we, and what's more, we have it in Monaco and Melbourne and Austria. When you walk into the paddock in Melbourne for the first race of the season it hits you what a wonderful environment you're in, simply because it's such a stunning paddock. Just seeing how much effort they put in to the hospitality and how luxurious it looks, how well every-thing is presented. It's like, *Whoa*. You've got the top team at the near end: Mercedes, followed by Ferrari and then Red Bull (the further you have to walk down the paddock, the further down the ranking you are).

I definitely enjoyed that, being a part of that scene. Just the look of it, for starters. Everything from the trailer to the garages is absolutely pristine. And the cars. I mean, you race in other cate-gories and the vehicles are often a bit banged up with scratches, stone chips and such, but there's not a mark, there's not a thumb-print or a grease smear on an F1 car. They're polished and buffed into flawless works of art, and because they're painted for every race they look that good every single time.

The whole thing about Formula One is that we put so much time and effort into the chase for perfection; everything is about detail, and as a result everything but everything, from the cars themselves to the teacups, looks a-mazing.

I think that's a huge part of the appeal. It's that escapism. Life isn't perfect, but Formula One is just about as close as we're going to get. And of course we as drivers benefit enormously from that reflected glamour. Unlike footballers, we don't have 20,000 people screaming rude things about our wives. I've got so much respect for football players in dealing with that aggression. I don't know how they do it, I really don't. And I hope I'm not tempting fate here, but in F1 we just haven't seen the kind of financial and sexual scandals that have dogged, say, football and boxing. There are fewer F1 drivers, of course, but even so there does seem to be a general feeling of the drivers behaving themselves – or at least misbehaving a bit more successfully – than footballers.

A lot of this is to do with the media. As a driver you're in front of the cameras a lot. The first person they speak to after a race is not the team manager, it's the driver, and you've got to be ready for that; you've got to understand that you're not just talking on behalf of yourself but the other 500 other people in the team. As a result I think you grow up very quickly, become more respectful. And if you're wondering how that fits in with this section's theme of glamour, well, it just does, because it's all about the global image of the sport, and upholding that image, and how we all do our bit towards it.

4. THE SPONSORS (AKA MORE 'THE MONEY')

In 1991, Alain Prost was turfed out of Ferrari halfway through a season for trash-talking his own team (he was also fired by Renault for the same reason at the end of the 1983 season). But aside from trash-talking, and getting truly appalling results, the other main reason you're likely to get your marching orders is if you upset a sponsor.

The thing is, it's not easy for any team in Formula One to exist; it costs a fortune – $200–$400 million a year – so if it came to a choice between the sponsor and the driver, then the team would get rid of the driver.

But it just doesn't happen now because everyone in Formula One knows on which side their bread is buttered. In other words, they're wise to the fact that the sponsors put money into the team, which in very real terms means the team can build a better, faster car, which in turn gives you a better chance of winning. The team can pay for the best drivers – not just the two up front, but better test drivers, too – they can pay for the better staff; they can spend more money on a wind tunnel. It's no coincidence that the two richest teams in F1, Mercedes and Ferrari, are also the two quickest teams in Formula One.

So in a very real sense you as the driver can use the sponsor – or, rather, the sponsorship situation – to your advantage. You understand that the sponsor wants you there. That you're integral to their interests in the team, and that if they liked another driver more then they'd probably sponsor that team instead. You being able to understand how the cogs of team, sponsor and driver interlink and that for it all to work you all have to be doing your job properly. Ultimately, the way a driver deals with the sponsor will be a key part of his longevity in the sport.

Am I good at it? Damn straight I am. I realised quite early on that it's important to be good in every area and schmoozing sponsors is definitely one of them. Plus I really enjoyed it because the people I was meeting were genuinely interested in Formula One. I'd always try not to ask boring questions. I would ask things about driving, put them on the spot a little bit, make them a little bit uncomfortable, and they loved it; I'd start a conversation as a friend would; it wouldn't be just like, 'Yeah, it's great to be here this weekend *blah blah blah*,' and all the boring stuff that you have to say. I'd try and make it a bit more personal, hopefully get the crowd laughing, take the piss out of myself or take the piss out of the marketing people I'm with, get a rise out of people. And I think that makes a difference, because they remember you; it's not just, 'Oh, some Formula One driver came in and did a little speech.' It's different, more personal.

Mind you, as a tactic it backfired a bit. Other drivers would turn up to sponsor events, be a bit distant and disinterested, do the guppy fish impression, and so the sponsor would ask for me next time, and I'd end up doing the lion's share.

It's the same with the media. I used to like having a laugh with the press, or at least having a laugh because of the press.

There was this one time, not at band camp – 2014, it was – when we were struggling with the car and my PR man, James Williamson, would get me to say certain words in my answer. It was just to amuse ourselves, really. We loved the Cookie Monster advert, where the Cookie Monster kept saying, 'How about now?' as he's waiting for the cookies to be ready. He keeps saying it. 'How about now? How about now?'

So there I was in a press conference in Canada, getting really cheesed off with the same old question, and in the end I said, 'This is really tough, you know, you keep asking me the same question about when is the performance going to get better, you keep saying, how about now? How about now? How about now?' And I kind of framed it as though I was losing my rag when unbeknown to anyone (apart from James, who I could hear laughing into his hand) it was just me doing a Cookie Monster impression.

Meanwhile, I was always taught when doing an interview to end on a positive, because that's what they remember. On one occasion in Montreal we were speaking to various McLaren high-ups, and I was being interviewed on stage by one of the team members. So the first thing I did was to take the piss out of the team member interviewing me. I went on to talk about how shit the day was and then I ended on a high: 'But tomorrow, I'm sure it's going to be fantastic with your support,' and just left them with a bit of positivity.

Did I ever get sick of being a walking sponsorship board? Yes and no. When you're paid that kind of money you should wear a diarrhoea-coloured frilly tutu if that's what they want. Yes, you have lots of demands on you and your time, and it's certainly not what you'd call an easy life. But it's so well remunerated that all other considerations have to come second. And after all, you always have the option to step aside if it all gets too much.

But on the other hand, maybe I did feel a little... *owned*. I was often aware that we were being used every second of our lives. Like if the public see you wearing a watch that isn't a sponsor's watch, they'll say, 'Hang on a sec, why is he wearing that watch and not the sponsor's watch?' and the sponsors will be, 'Shit, this is an issue. He prefers that other watch,' and before you know it you'll have people on the phone treating it like a major diplomatic incident when the fact is you just picked up the wrong watch on your way out to fetch a coffee.

Same if I was papped somewhere and I was in a BMW when I drove for Honda. I wouldn't go back to the car. I'd leave it until I knew that the paps had gone.

Still, whatever I'm advertising, I try my best to do it well, even if I know it's shit. You couldn't refuse to be sponsored, as such, but I would say to the team that I'm not doing certain things, and in my contract there are some things that I will and won't do.

For example, the sponsor can't use me and just me; they had to have the car in the background and had to have a racing element to the photo they use for advertising. Little details like that. So it wasn't solely me as an individual sponsoring a brand that I might not want to associate myself with.

For Honda I'm an ambassador, which means I do 'ambassadorial' things for them. Again, there's a line. Like if they wanted me to frolic on a beach with buxom beauties or something equally crass I could refuse. But I also know that they wouldn't do that because Honda is a brand that is very respectful, so it's good working with them.

I went to Australia to do a one-day, which was just about the most fun sponsor event ever. They flew me out there, I drove a Civic-type car around Bathurst, which is a beautiful circuit up in the mountains. All I had to do was set the lap record for a front-wheel-drive road car, one that hadn't been set yet. So I just went out and had fun, had a few beers in the evening and came home, and that was it.

Compare that to 2010, the first year of McLaren – or 'Vodafone McLaren Mercedes' as the press kit had me say – when I'd come from Brawn to join Lewis. McLaren had the previous two World Champions racing as teammates, and boy were they going to make the most of it. They used us every day on sponsor events. Race weekends were packed with photo-ops; they were pulling us out of engineering meetings to do sponsor events. We were like, 'Guys, we understand the need to do marketing and interviews, but our priority is making the car go faster.'

Lewis was lucky, because my manager, Richard, did all the fighting on behalf of us both, and it remains the only time I've ever complained about too much work in F1. Marketing

listened, of course, and as result scaled the promotional appear-
ances right back.

For about, oh, a fortnight.

5. THE SPENDING

Coming into F1, I had no idea what I was doing, especially when
it came to money, and my manager at the time, a thoroughly
lovely bloke, if a little green, said, 'It's fine, you've got a long
career ahead of you, spend it!'

I'm not blaming him. He was himself a multi-millionaire businessman. He just wanted me to be happy and I was all too willing
to take his advice. So I bought a house as well as the expensive
apartment I was renting in Monaco, and I also bought…

Cars and motorhomes

The trick is to buy a limited car – but don't sell it right away.
You get people who buy and sell them straight away but Ferrari
and other manufacturers don't like it when you do that, so you're
probably not going to get your hands on a limited-edition Ferrari
ever again. On the other hand, it's the people who buy and sell
instantly who tend to make the most money on them.

One thing I do know, however, is that the richest man is the
one who buys a Ferrari that's not limited. You buy a Ferrari that's
not limited, you drive it out off the forecourt and it's dropped
$50,000 already and that's the richest man in the world who does

that – who doesn't care about losing that money. Whereas I will only buy a car if I know it's a limited car, because I'll hold on to my money.

Other things I spent a lot of money on: a motorhome. Argh! I remember the conversation with Richard. I said, 'I don't know if I can do this any longer,' and he was, like, 'Well, why don't you try making it as easy on yourself as possible? Get rid of some of your peripheral worries so that you can relax and stay focused on the race…'

He would be proved correct. Although I've bought a lot of things that have cost me a small fortune, mostly they were all about making my life easier so that I could continue in Formula One for longer.

My motorhome (in the end, motorhomes, plural) was a prime example. It felt like home. I'd get back from the circuit, whether it was a good day or a bad day, walk in and be like, 'Ah, a restful oasis away from the circus of Formula One.' I'd open the fridge and gaze upon my Babybels (my beloved Babybels) as well as all the rest of my food. I had my kettle, my bed…

Of course it's got a bed, you're thinking. *What sort of shonky motorhome doesn't have a bed?* But the point is that it was *my* bed. When you stay in a hotel, not only do you play a bed version of Russian roulette – because even the best hotels can have shit beds – but it also takes a while to get used to what you've got. Even if it's a great bed it's still a couple of nights before you've adjusted to it and start getting proper restful sleep.

Having a motorhome meant I no longer had the bed problem. In fact, it meant I no longer had hotel issues at all. I could only use it for European races, but that was ideal, because a lot of European hotels were a bit on the average side and were situated a bit too near the circuit, meaning you'd often get fans and media hanging around outside.

My motorhome, on the other hand, with its Babybels and its comfortable, familiar bed, was always parked somewhere secret. They weren't allowed in the circuit so we had to find somewhere else to park nearby – although I say 'we', when, happily, it wasn't my problem to find out where the motorhome should go. I had a driver. My driver would be driving the motorhome across Europe as I flew. Then at the race he'd get a hotel as I stayed in the motorhome. A great arrangement, but, of course, expensive. You're paying for your flights, you're paying for getting the motorhome to the races, you're paying for staying in the motorhome, because you have to pay for security, you have to pay for where it's parked, and you're paying for the driver's hotel as well.

So the cost was just unreal every race. And that's on top of the price of the motorhome, which for a top-of-the-range Newell, who are one of the best people who make motorhomes, could be $1m, $1.5m.

At Brawn, it was myself and my teammate, Rubens Barrichello, who both had the same type of motorhome, the aforementioned Newell. Sebastian had one. Fernando had one. Nico Rosberg had one. Lewis has (or had) a truck, which was bigger inside, but not as luxurious, very contemporary. I didn't like it – it didn't feel like home. Cool, but not to my taste. So that was probably six or seven of us who had motorhomes, and so we all clubbed together to pay for a 'motorhome guy' who would make sure our motorhomes were clean and that they were stocked with Babybels and that the bed was set up at night so you didn't have to do it yourself. I ask you. Talk about pampered.

During testing, the circuit relaxed its rules on having motorhomes so you could have it in the paddock, which meant you could cross from the garage, across the paddock and go straight into your motorhome. So cool.

The first one I had used to belong to Mika Salo, and Jacques Villeneuve before him. It had a leopard-skin print theme running through the interior and looked a bit like a gin palace, which was no doubt what had enchanted both Mika and Jacques. Apart from a weird sink-next-to-the-bed bit of negative feng shui it was great, but even so, the time came to trade up.

My next one used to belong to the NASCAR driver Jimmy Johnson and was 45 feet long, just about as big as you can get. In fact, it was so big that it was illegal to register it in the UK, so I had to register it in Ireland. It had a lounge area, kitchen in the middle, bedrooms at the back.

There's so much that can go wrong with them. Even more than with a boat, which is surprising. A lot of them have hydraulic pull-outs to make the rooms bigger, only they go wrong and then water comes in and you get mould. The shower will pack up.

You'll fix that and something else will break. You're throwing money away like a man with three arms.

I sold it after I finished in F1. I bought it for $400,000 and sold it for $130,000. Lovely thing to have, but I must say I breathed a sigh of relief when it was gone.

Yachts

I bought a boat I couldn't afford. I earned half a million dollars a year and it cost £800,000, so I was immediately in debt.

Yachts, you probably don't need me to tell you, are expensive to buy and they're expensive to run. Mine was moored at Monaco harbour, which isn't cheap, plus you need to employ a captain to live on it, keep everything – yes – shipshape, and tell you when you need a new engine, which I did at one point. Again: not cheap. This guy would never see me. Three weeks a year I was on that boat, at most, and I ended up chartering it out because I just couldn't afford to run it, what with paying for him, the repairs, harbour fees and, oh, God, fuel – fuel is *unbelievably* expensive. I remember when I picked up my first boat, *Little Missy*, in 2001, I invited my mates from Frome over for a holiday and one day they said, 'Right, JB, today we're going to pay for the fuel for the boat.'

I was, like, 'No, it's okay, it's fine, it's fine.'

'No, no we're going to sort it out.'

I was, like, 'Guys, seriously, you don't have to…'

They said, 'Come on, come on. How much is it going to be?'

I said, 'Two and a half grand to fill it up.'

'Okay,' they said, 'How about we, sort of, pay a bit towards it? Like, a hundred pounds...'

In all, the yacht was costing me hundreds of thousands of dollars a year.

And I ended up buying two.

Little Missy was 20 metres. I got rid of that one and bought a new one, *Ichiban*, in 2014. That one cost £5,000–£6,000 to fill up with fuel and was 28 metres long, which isn't all that big when you consider that back in the day Eddie Irvine had a 100-foot boat; Jacques Villeneuve's was 145-foot.

Someone will always have a bigger boat, that's what they say. It doesn't matter how much money you've got and how much money you spend on a yacht, someone will always have a bigger one. They also say that the best boat is your mate's boat, and that's just as true.

Still, it was really stunning, that second boat: *Ichiban*. It had four bedrooms, slept eight people. We took it to Sardinia, Corsica, the Italian coast, the French Riviera, sailed it down the coast to St-Tropez.

The living area had a sheer glass wall giving you a beautiful view of the ocean, and as for stocking it, we filled it full of alcohol, lots of rosé. That was our drink of choice. Rosé and beer were the must-haves on the boat. I had a chef, who was amazing. She'd be on the boat six months of the year, along with the captain and a first mate. I'm not sure what they were all doing – cleaning, I suppose, and taking out the jet ski and paddle board to make sure they were in working order. Enjoying the luxury of yacht life in Monaco, knowing that I was paying them to do it. Oh God.

At least I could be certain they weren't having wild parties on my dollar. My captain kept a tight ship. Nobody was allowed to get near the boat if they were smoking a cigarette. Even my friends, if they had a cigarette, he'd be cross with them. He was in his forties, while the rest of the crew were in their twenties and he ruled over them with the proverbial rod of iron.

Mainly, I loved it and had some great times on it. The trouble is that however much fun you're having, you're super-aware of the sheer amount of money you're throwing away. They say it's like having a bag of cash and the whole time you're on the boat, chucking $100 bills into the ocean, and it's true. But I enjoyed it and I loved being on the water. Yes, I probably should have just chartered a boat when I fancied it. But hindsight is a wonderful thing.

Planes

Confession: this bit's a cheat, because I didn't actually buy a plane. Thank God. Back in the day, people were spending a fortune on them. It was the proper glitzy, glamorous lifestyle of an F1 playboy: planes, cars and boats. Rubens Barrichello had one, Michael Schumacher, Eddie Irvine. Lewis had one for years but sold it. Why? Surprise, surprise, it turns out that you're throwing money away when you own a plane. Worse even than boats.

Just for starters, if you're going to buy a new one and you want it capable of making transatlantic flights – which of course you would if you're a Formula One driver – it's going to cost you $20 million plus, and it'll be no comfier than flying first class. Then you need a crew. Then you have airport fees, and of course the dreaded aviation fuel. Plus, if you own a plane you're going to have to service it, and when you're servicing it for those three or four weeks, you're going to have to rent another plane.

All of which means that if you have to fly private then it's better to rent, and what a lot of drivers ended up doing was clubbing together to rent a private jet so it cost us less.

We'd fly to Russia on a 14-seater jet and share the cost, which would be about £4,000 each. It's a pretty good way to travel, because you're not queuing up, and if you take a nap you haven't got people gawping at you while you're asleep, which has always struck me as a bit unsettling when I'm flying. Like, what if I start drooling, or do one of those weird sleep-spasms when I'm drifting off?

Saying that, the interior of a private jet – or a PJ as we call them, being simply too spoiled to say the words out in full – isn't actually that grand. Not unless you get a really big one. A lot of people will climb aboard a private jet and go, 'God, it's so small in here,' possibly because they hadn't been paying attention when they took a look from the outside, or were maybe expecting a TARDIS-like interior. Get a load of racing drivers onboard, all of whom are in an over-caffeinated state, either because they're excited about the race ahead or excited about a week away from the circus, and things can even start to feel a little bit cramped, not to mention a bit farty. Like a lot of things, it's often better in theory than it is in reality.

6. THE TRAVEL

Travelling is glamorous. Even though it isn't, because it's long and tiring and boring, it sort of is anyway. *Just is.* And as drivers we don't take it for granted, because we know we're doing cool stuff that most people will never get to experience. Going to Australia once a year is awesome, for example. And then you go to Japan, wicked. And then Brazil. A lot of these countries I never would have thought about going to it, if I wasn't racing in F1.

Travel Tips From The Long-Haul Expert

Airlines

These days. I do plenty of flying to Japan plus to the Grand Prix for my work with Sky. In all I do close to 16 long-haul flights a year. I fly business, not first class, and although I fly with all sorts of airlines, I've definitely got it down to the best ones now, and weirdly enough, considering that they're usually on the end of a bad-PR story and it's difficult to find someone with a good word to say about them, Delta is the best airline if you're flying to Japan.

For a start, it's a brand-new plane, the Airbus 350. Now, all planes fly the same 'actual' altitude, around 31,000 feet, but internally they don't, of course; they're pressurised to a lower altitude. And while most normal planes are internally pressurised to 6,000 feet, an A350 flies at about 4,500 feet internally, which means the passengers get less tired. As a result, I really do feel less fatigued when I get off an Airbus 350.

And Delta's the only company that fly them and they're brand new inside. Plus in business class, you get a door, so it's proper fun. It's like a little suite.

Don't take luggage

I never take anything, except hand luggage, so I save up to an hour checking in luggage at one end and then collecting it at the other end. Bo-ho-nus.

Check in online

And you can check in online, so you can arrive less than an hour before the flight leaves and still be on time. All that stuff about making sure you're at the airport three hours before your flight? Pah.

Get on 'local' time

As soon as you arrive on the plane, you should already be thinking of yourself as being at your destination. So if you get on a plane in LA and it's 1pm, you should already think that you're on Japanese time, which is 16 hours in front, thus it's five in the morning there, and you should sleep and eat accordingly.

So, if I get on the plane at 1pm, I try to sleep immediately and then after about six hours, wake up, because then it will be 11am in Japan. Literally, I get on the plane and that's it. Everyone's eating and I'm earplugs in, eye mask on, getting some shut-eye.

There are certain flights out of LA that work and some flights that don't. Some flights take off at midnight, others at 10 in the morning, but the midnight flights are better because I arrive in Japan at 5am and I've slept for a whole night.

Be a mathematician about it

Japan is 16 hours ahead of me in Los Angeles, so to work it out I move the current time forward one day and then move it back eight hours. Coming back is weird, because I take a midnight flight after the race on Sunday and arrive home at 5pm on Sunday. Marty McFly has nothing on me.

But don't think about the time back home

The thing is, my body now knows LA as 'home' and lets me get straight back on my home time zone quickly. So coming this way is not too bad.

Going the other way – out to Japan – however, is really tough, and I've found the best if not only policy is just not to think about the fact that if I want to go to Japan I lose two days of my life. Just gone, just like that.

Take Melatonin

Don't look so alarmed. Melatonin is what you produce when you're tired. So it's all natural and all you're doing by taking a supplement is adding to it a little bit. Just giving it a wee boost. I normally take 5mg. I always take it when I travel. And I take it as soon as I get on board. It takes 15 minutes to work, and it's a nice sleep, because you don't wake up groggy. Just helps you drift off.

Don't drink to excess

They say you shouldn't drink at all, but I find it's nice to have that little glass of red. I'll probably have it in the lounge before I get on board, though. Don't tell anyone.

Keep yourself busy

If, like me, you're on your own from when you leave home until you arrive at your destination, you'll want something to do en route: a film to watch, a book or a couple of magazines to read. Whatever you do, make it an activity that's absorbing but not too demanding. Something you know will keep you occupied for long hours on end. Personally, I'm a big one for watching a box set on my laptop.

Sleep

Once you've found the right bed, hold onto it tight. Don't let it go. I've spent a lot of time in the Grand Hyatt in Tokyo and I love their beds and pillows, so every time I land in Japan, I stay there for the night before we go off to the race.

Late last year, I had some flowers and a letter from them that said, 'Congratulations, Mr Button, you've stayed with us 50 times,' which was nice. I've probably stayed with them about 80 times now, which has got me wondering what'll happen when I get to 100.

7. OFF-SEASON

Generally speaking, drivers go their own way during the off-season. You never hang out with a racing driver in the winter. Daniel Ricciardo would go home to Australia, Lewis would go to LA; me, I used to go to Hawaii on holiday, because it was the only break I really had throughout the year.

During the mid-season break I'd go to either Ibiza or St-Tropez for two weeks, and I remember that being weird, because I'd feel fine and then at the end of the break, like literally the last day of the holiday I'd be all blocked up, get a cold and be poorly for another week leading up to the next race. That probably happened for about two years on the trot, before I was like, 'Hey, guys, maybe we'll go to St-Tropez for one week, not two.'

Hawaii, then, in the off-season. Apart from relaxing I'd do a lot of fitness training. Every year you'd get a little bit fitter and do a little bit more, and for me, the perfect place to do that was Hawaii. I'd train in the morning and most afternoons, spend the rest of the day lazing around, have a few drinks and then get back to training the next day.

Being in Hawaii meant that I missed Christmas with the family, but I think they understood that I needed time to relax and get away from the world of motor racing. Well, they said they understood. I don't know if they really did. I haven't asked them since. I know my mum missed me not being there, but I've made up for it, because in the last few years, since I've been with Brit, we go home every year to see everyone and it's really, really nice to have a big family affair. Just brilliant to see my three sisters, and all of their kids. It's a massive get-together.

After off-season, I would always struggle to get back in the car. After a winter of living a different kind of life – a more relaxing, me-time sort of life, it took time. But as soon as I got back in the groove I could think about nothing else. I was a man obsessed. I couldn't switch off. Again, it was another reason I ended up pulling the plug for good.

The highest-paid sportsmen of all time, by the way, is Gaius Appuleius Diocles, a Roman chariot racer who earned 35,863,120 sesterces, which when adjusted for inflation amounts to well over $15 billion.

DOING
THE JOB

Racecraft is the basis of all racing. It's how to overtake, how to brake, how to position your car correctly when you're fighting for position; it's about understanding racing lines and using your skill and instinct to find the quickest way around a circuit.

It's also about dealing with the extra stuff that gets thrown at you. Like the weather doesn't do what it's supposed to do. Or maybe the car you're driving doesn't suit your style and you need to change up – in which case, you either adapt your style of racing to suit the car, or adapt the car to suit your racing style.

My driving style is, in a word, smooth. I try to drive as though I'm racing a 60cc go-kart. I like to brake and carry speed through a corner; I like to judge the racing line. Precision. That's what it's all about for me. I began that way in karting and – with a bit of necessary fine-tuning – carried it through to F1. I like to think I continue it now in Super GT.

I'm the same in a road car. Smooth as a pint of Guinness. Mind you, Brittny would have a thing or two to say about that. She thinks I brake too late, pulling up to the car in front, and while that's technically true, it's also fine because I might brake late but I don't brake hard, and that's because I don't want people's heads doing the nodding-dog thing in the passenger seat.

But, yes, fair cop. We do get close to the car in front and that's Britt's issue. Late and soft – that's me.

A lot depends on what you're driving. When I'm in her G-Wagen, it's like a bucking bronco anyway, which is why I prefer to take the BMW 5 Series, because I can't be dealing with driving around LA feeling like I'm doing that scene in *Wayne's World* where they're all head-banging in the car.

But anyway. When it comes to driving, that's how I roll. The drawback is that if I'm in a racing car that doesn't handle the way I want it to, I won't be as quick as the likes of Lewis or Fernando, because I'm not one who can wring a car's neck the way they can. If they're driving a car with too much front grip, for example, they'll be better at adapting to that than me. If you have too much front grip, the rear slides throughout, and I hate that feeling. Not to get all *Carry On Formula One Driver* about it, but I need a firm rear, matron. I need it stable so I can take that speed through a corner. A tiny bit of front sliding, that's fine, because I know where to put the car at the corner, just as long as I can have confidence in my rear. And if I have that, and if I can fine-tune the car so that it works with my style, then I'm unbeatable.

I was always better in the wet. I've won 15 Grand Prix, and I reckon nine of them were wet. The reason is that I can feel the unusual conditions and I can really think on my feet or, in my case my bum, because that's how I feel the car.

A lot of drivers struggle in the wet. They'll look at the circuit and they'll go, 'Well, it's a bit slippy in that corner, so I'll slow down,' whereas me, I like to arrive at the corner and decide on the fly, feeling the corner through the car and through the tyres, and that's how I always gain time in those tricky conditions of when it gets wet through a race or if it dries out through a race and you're on slightly the wrong tyre, so you could be in the wet on a dry tyre and I can always find the grip, whereas a lot of people can't.

I know that that's what frustrated Fernando when Lewis started in F1 as his teammate at McLaren. At the start of their partnership (if you can ever call teammates in F1 a partnership), Fernando would destroy Lewis, but Lewis would look at the data and do a bit of Sherlock Hamilton: *Oh, Fernando's braking there. Okay, I'm going to brake there. Fernando's accelerating there. Okay, I'll accelerate there.*

And although by rights it shouldn't be as easy as that, it somehow was for Lewis, so he'd just hammer the brakes where he thought was right: 100-metre board, bang, brakes, turn in, come out, and be as quick as Fernando.

Not quicker. But *as* quick. And this would bother Fernando. And because of that, and because Lewis got inside his head, Fernando made more mistakes, which Lewis didn't, because he was the new boy, had no pressure, could make mistakes and no one cared. Whereas for double World Champion Fernando it was different. And Lewis ended up being quicker.

So yes, drivers definitely learn – even poach – from each other in terms of style, although it's more to do with hard facts than technique, like you'll see from the data that so-and-so has taken a corner flat. *Hmm*, you'll think, *I didn't think it was quite flat through that corner, but he's done it, so it must be okay,* or *He's able to go flat there, but I'm not, so why is that? What's different about his car?* which sends you back to looking at the set-ups. *Ah, he's got more rear wing, maybe I should try more rear wing…*

Learning. See? It always comes back to that. Which brings me onto…

1. STARTS

My first pole position in Formula One was at the San Marino Grand Prix at Imola in 2004. I'm in my BAR-Honda. I'm 24 years old. Just behind me is the World Champion Michael Schumacher in a Ferrari.

No pressure, then.

So I pull up to the start and over the radio my racing engineers tell me, 'Right, JB, time to do the procedure.'

Which is the start procedure.

And it's like that moment you're at the cash machine, go to plug in your PIN and suddenly can't remember it. Or when you walk into the shop needing a pint of milk and your mind goes blank.

I've just achieved my first-ever pole position. I'm ahead of Michael Schumacher, and I've forgotten how to start the bloody car. It's arming the launch control – a procedure I've done dozens, no, *hundreds* of times. All year I've done it in the simulator, in practice and testing, so much so that it's virtually a case of muscle memory.

Except that it's gone.

And the lights are coming on, and normally the procedure should have begun by now and I'm thinking, *Shit what do I do?* I'm looking at the lights and I'm going all hot and fizzy and then *boom* it comes back and *bam, bam, bam*, I do the procedure, and pull away as the lights go out and...

Have the best start of my life.

Proper good. I must pull four car lengths ahead of Michael (who goes on to beat me into second, but still).

Despite the fact that I got a good start, it was more by luck than judgement, and it's not something I'd wish to repeat in a hurry. You can be fast in testing and practice, you can ace qualifying, you can be as quick as possible. But if you get your start wrong, you can lose two or three places, and if you're at the front of the grid and you lose places you find yourself caught up in traffic, and that can be disastrous. A good start isn't just desirable, it's essential, and as a result it's something we practise in the simulator a lot. Apart from rolling it in to the harbour, much of those two simulator days prior to Monaco were spent on my starts. (And then what happened? I ended up starting from the pits anyway.)

What we call the start procedure begins way before that moment I've just described and involves doing a lot of prep beforehand. To make sure the clutch is working and warmed up correctly, you do what's called a 'clutch bite point find', which is a case of understanding where the bite point is for when you release the hand clutch at the start, because that bit's still manual. It's the only clutch use that's manual, because the only time we use the clutch paddles – there are two, usually – is for the start and for pit stops. For gear changes, it's another paddle and it's all done automatically.

Next, you do your tyre warm-up where the team has told you how many burnouts to do, because they know what temperature the tyres are at and what temperature they should be. You achieve a burnout by accelerating in first gear and spinning the wheels. The car has 900 horsepower, and each burnout will raise your tyre temperature by around six degrees. Usually, you're asked to do four of them, the last one being just before you stop on the grid.

When you stop, although you'll get less tyre temperature on the surface, it will still be there internally, and then you're basically sitting there twiddling your thumbs, waiting for the rest of the grid to queue up. Hopefully, you're waiting a long time for them to form up, because that means you're at the front, which is fine – so fine, in fact, that you don't even worry about losing tyre temperature, because after all it's the same for everyone around you, and even though those at the back have warmer tyres it's not like they're going to overtake you. Well, hopefully not. Nope. You're just glad you're at the front. Open track – that's what you want.

Next it's announced that all cars are formed up, at which point you get ready to launch. All the way through my career it's been different: between 2001 and 2003 we had a system called launch control, where you'd release the clutch, and then when the lights started coming on, go full throttle with your foot on the brake, *ba, ba, ba, ba, ba, ba.* And then, when the lights went out, you'd push a button and the car just *went* – it did everything as it should. Benetton were very good at that. They'd often make two or three places up at the start, just because of their brilliant launch control.

After the launch control era we had a manual system, and for this we had the two clutch paddles I'm talking about. What you'd do was pull up, put it in gear, stick your finger behind one clutch and pull it to about 60 per cent while pulling the other clutch paddle all the way in. Then you'd sit there, revving up to, say, 8,000rpm, waiting, the noise around you like the sound of the planet splitting open even with your earplugs in, an absolutely astonishing, primal-sounding noise.

And then the lights would go out and – *boom* – you'd dump the fully retracted clutch immediately, so you'd still have a large percentage of clutch not engaged as you pulled away, at which point you'd hear a beep and then release the second clutch fully and start going heavy on the throttle.

So that was pretty fancy. But then they banned that, so you'd have to find a way of doing the start with just one pedal, where you'd pull the clutch in, get the revs right, the lights would go out and then you'd release the clutch, it would hit your fingers, you'd hold it at about 50 per cent and then at the beep release it completely.

It sounds needlessly complicated, and it probably is. Most of all, it's weird and funky trying to get your fingers in the right position, but it's what you have to do, because that's the best way to get a good start. Clutch control is paramount and getting your fingers in the right place is the first battle. After that it's difficult to explain and tough to understand unless you're actually sitting in the car – and even then it's something that happens more by instinct, feel and racing mojo than anything else. Although you're using different equipment and manipulating it differently, the principle is the same as it is in a road car: you know when you know. Ever tried to teach someone clutch control? If so, you'll know what I mean. It's all done by feel.

As far as the throttle goes, you're told which revs to use, so you'll have lights on the wheel, which are programmed to respond to your throttle use, and the idea is to get the lights to meet in the middle of the wheel, which means you've hit the throttle sweet spot. Over to one side, too much throttle; over to another side, too little throttle. If you're 5 per cent out on the clutch pedal, you get a really bad start. Ditto if you react slowly. One-tenth late in a reaction works out to a loss of about 1.5 metres, and that's a killer.

There's so much else that can go wrong, too. Maybe somebody else has messed up their own start and stopped in front of you, which means you've got to turn the wheel and back off the throttle and that's the worst thing you can do, because when you go back on and you get a massive amount of wheel spin, or maybe you've released the paddles too quickly, you don't release them quickly enough, or you've come on the throttle too aggressively, or you've shifted up too early or too late...

In short, perfecting a start is not easy, but it's those who make it look easy who end up doing the best. We've seen it in 2019 with the two Mercedes drivers: Valtteri Bottas has a bad start Lewis overtakes him and vice versa. In Barcelona, Bottas was on pole, had a poor start, Lewis ended up overtaking him and won.

So, if you were to ask me what the most important part of the whole weekend is, I'd be tempted to say qualifying but I'd be equally tempted to say the start, and then I'd settle on qualifying and change my mind the following day.

The eternal tyre conundrum

Tyres make a difference, of course. Soft or medium? A soft tyre will give you a six-metre advantage, meaning you'll be six metres quicker reaching 100kms an hour. However, the medium tyre is a better race tyre. So you, your race engineer and the strategists are faced with the decision: do you play the long game and go for the medium tyres, or decide to start with soft, knowing that on the soft you have a better chance of overtaking at the start, which is the easiest place to overtake? This, my friend, is what's known as a variable.

Easy on the throttle

You always have to be gentle with the throttle. Be anything other than gentle and the wheels will spin. The trick is to apply it slowly, and if you go on and get wheelspin, you lift off a bit and then go back on even more gently.

The good thing is that in a Formula One car we have a throttle map. A throttle maps is set of values applied to the throttle use that will change the behaviour of the throttle, depending on the driver's preference.

You can change the throttle map depending on the conditions. In the wet, for example, you'd adjust it to be a little less sensitive when you first apply the throttle, because otherwise you'd come out of a corner, touch the throttle and be in danger of losing the rear end of the car.

In the dry we play around with it. If you want you can have it mapped as a straight line all through the pedal, as it would be in a road car. But the way you'd normally have it in an F1 car is a little bit soft at first – that initial touch – so you can really get a feel for where the throttle pedal is. And that would be the first 20 per cent of your map, after which it would start picking up more aggressively and that's when you get the torque and power.

It's as much of an art form as using the brakes. For me, it's exactly the same in terms of modulation. I'm sure that Lewis, for example, would probably say that skill on the throttle comes second to using the brakes. But that's me. You're always working the throttle in tandem with the brakes. You're dancing with them both, modulating both at the same time. Well, I am, because that's my style. Other drivers are very different.

Pole, turn one

Always best to start on pole, I find. The only thing is that you may find yourself vulnerable to an overtake at turn one. The guy behind can tow up to you all the way down the straight, sit behind you and, come turn one, may well be able to have a run at you.

That's what happened to me in 2009, racing for Brawn in Barcelona. I had started on pole, with Sebastian second in a Red Bull and my teammate Rubens Barrichello third. Off we went at lights out, and my start was fine, but Rubens' was better, allowing him to pass Sebastian then tow up to me and pass me on turn one. Fortunately, I went on to win thanks to a different pit-stop strategy (more on that in pit stops).

So, yes. In terms of Sunday, the actual race itself, the start and turn one are the most important. Stringing that particular one–two together can help make up for a bad qualifying session, because if you're starting eighth on the grid and you get to turn one and suddenly everyone's on the inside, you can take advantage of the inevitable bottleneck by coming around the outside, capitalising on the fact that they're all slowing down in heavy traffic, and drive down the outside. You can brake later, going round and make up positions.

Then next year it's different. Maybe the outside was good for an overtake last year, but this year, for some reason, everyone's on the outside, so the inside's better. Maybe two cars touch, and because they touch the guys behind are nervous of crashing, lift off, and that slows everyone down, and again because you're further back you can take the other side and make up positions.

Having said all that, there really is no substitute for being up the front, because if you've qualified, say, tenth, there's a much bigger chance you're going to crash. Fourteenth is the worst. When you're right at the back you can hang back and see what's going on. But when you're 14th, you don't want to lose places to the cars behind, so you've got to push and you try and overtake which means there's a big chance of crashing or damaging the car.

Both of these are bad. Crashing is bad, obviously. But damaging the car is even worse. If somebody drives into the back of you and damages your floor or your diffuser, it's a lot of downforce gone, but you can still carry on, and it's the worst indignity – up there with taking out your teammate and being overtaken on the outside. You're just driving Miss Daisy for an hour and a half, wishing that you'd crashed and were in the wall, because at least that would be better than what you're doing now, being lapped and cursing your terrible start.

2. GEARS

In a racing car, you're changing down as you come into the corner, which is what you should be doing in any car, except most people don't think to change down. They get to the corner, go to accelerate, realise there's no power and *then* change down gears.

In an F1 car, your braking and shifting go together, with one being a reaction to the other. You're coming into a third-gear corner in eighth, which in an F1 car is top gear, so it's brake then *shift, shift, shift, shift, shift.* There's a safety mechanism fitted so that you can't shift down by too much and over-rev the engine. It'll only let you shift down when it knows that the revs won't go above 12,500rpm.

You know which gear you need to be in for each corner. At Monaco, for example, there are three first-gear corners. Having said that, it's not like you have them memorised. I mean, you know from previous experience, and you're told, and you have all the data in front of you before you go out. But you get out there and it all happens by feel anyway.

Plus, it's often the case that gears can change from practice to qualifying. Say you have a corner, and you've been practising in third gear on old tyres, you might give it a go in fourth in qualifying because you've got new tyres, you've got less fuel, there's more grip on the circuit. It's a risk because you might screw it up by going in fourth, but you might be another tenth quicker. Again, that comes with feel and instinct.

Journos would always ask me after a race what gear I was in for such-and-such a corner, and I'd be like, 'Hmm, I think it was third, or it might have been fourth,' because as a driver it doesn't really matter, it's about listening to the car. Like if you feel the revs are too low, you downshift. If you feel that it's not going to pull when you get to the exit, or if it's pushing too much, and you need more engine braking, then it means that you're in too high a gear.

The whole process gives you a lot to do. You'll be changing as you're coming into the corner, and, at the same time, you're hammering on the brake and hitting the throttle, with most of the downshift taking place when you're still braking, and at the same time trying to balance the car when you shift that last gear. You're doing all of this at 200 miles an hour, remember. And if you're testing or qualifying then you're also trying to take note of how the car feels, so that you can relay it to the team afterwards.

A lot of people can't get their heads round this, but it's one of the reasons why a race is so much easier – or, I should say, less mentally taxing – than qualifying and even practice. It's because feedback's not an issue. You don't have to worry about what you're going to tell the team so you have more headspace to focus on your driving.

Either way, there are a lot of mental gymnastics involved, which is why it cracks me up when people say, 'Oh we should bring back stick gear shifts.' Yeah, right.

Go to the other extreme, and in 2001 all the teams had automatic gearboxes. It was all worked out on a computer and engineered so that it would shift down to certain gears on certain corners, but giving you, the driver, the leeway to override and change gear yourself if you fancied it for whatever reason. It was a bit weird to drive but I didn't mind it because you still had ultimate control. Still, they got rid of it.

One last point. The gear shift is on the paddles, of course, and you can design how skinny you want it to be, how far away from the steering wheel, how thick it should be, do all of that. It's great. You make it personal.

3. THE ANATOMY OF BRAKING

If, at high speed in a road car, you brake as hard as you can, you still won't slow down as much as you will just by lifting off in a Formula One car. Forget touching the brakes. Just lifting off. And that's all down to engine braking and our old friend down-force. Just lifting off you pull 1.5G. Hit the brakes as well and you're going up to 5G.

My left foot

And you'll be doing it with your left foot. Right foot is throttle, left foot is brake. And for me my left leg works just fine as a braking leg, which if you're a road car user might sound weird. I'm just used to it, because in F1, it's always been left-foot braking.

I can't get enough power with my right foot either, because it's just not used to putting that much power through the pedals, it's only done the throttle pedal before.

Conversely, a brake pedal on a road car is a lot more sensitive. They're not carbon brakes, so when you touch a road car pedal, you don't have to brake very hard. Like if I were to do it with my left foot, I'd brake too hard, I'd be through the windscreen. Whereas, my left leg in a race car can control and modulate a lot of power well. Even though you need to use a lot of power on the left leg I have so much feeling with it. I can't get the feedback I want from a road car.

In the zone

People say, 'Can you compare an F1 to a road car?' No, you can't, it's completely different. Gears, steering, acceleration, balance, behaviour, everything. And of all those areas, the one that's most pronounced is braking. Most people don't understand why the brake pedal in a racing car is so hard. People get into F1 cars, reach turn one and go straight on because they didn't realise they had to hit it so hard. It's a very different feeling to your road car.

The first stab of the brake is the most important, because that's when you have the most downforce at the highest speed and thus when you get the most braking force and pull the highest G. So that first hit is massively important in slowing the car down. If you arrive in the braking zone and you push it gently you won't be taking advantage of the downforce and you won't be stopping at the rate you need. Fine for a warm-up lap, perhaps, but not in a racing scenario.

Now, normally, if the tyres are up to temperature and you hit the brakes hard you won't lock up. But if the tyres are not in their working range – so they're a bit old or not at the correct temperature – then you'll lock up. It's what happens when you hit the brakes and the pads grab the disk. The front tyre locks and they smoke. That's just carbon brakes for you, really. They're very grabby until they're up to temperature. And it'll happen if the brakes are too cold, or if the car hits the ground as you brake because you're running the wrong ride height or the tyre pressure is too low. You'll hit the brakes, the front will hit the ground, you lock up, you've lost time, you've probably damaged the tyre and run wide. You messed up.

Brake dance

So, you've got to hit it hard and then after the initial hit, you back off. You shouldn't ever hit the brake and then come off and then go back on, because if you're doing that it means you've misjudged the entrance to the corner and you don't want to do that because that's BAD.

The perfect scenario is to hit the brake hard, come off the brake gradually, then turn in and go back on the throttle. If it's a hairpin and you've done it right, you should be able to just hammer the brake, turn and then gradually apply the throttle, but mainly you're constantly judging your footwork. Like during a race, when the tyres are getting old, you'll be prone to a bit of oversteer on entry, so you'll be using the brakes to balance the car all the way to the apex, then turn and exit.

Things go south if you brake too late. Normally, as I say, you have the first hit on the brakes and then slowly come off the brakes. But if you've braked too late, you hit the brakes and not only are you on the pedal for longer but you have to turn in while you're braking, and at that point you've got problems, because when you brake in a straight line, the whole surface of the tyre is on the ground and everything's fine. But when you turn and brake, there's camber, which means there's less of the tyre actually touching the road, and if you brake hard and turn in, you're likely to lose grip, lock up the inside unweighted front, damage the tyre and go straight on.

It's different with different types of tyres: Michelin, you can brake and turn in a little bit more, Bridgestone, you can't. You've got to wait until you've done the braking and then turn in. So you really need to understand the tyres that you're on as well.

Brake wait

It's crucial to get your braking right, because it sets up the whole corner. You need to be brave on the brakes and have confidence in the car. You need to have confidence in yourself. You need to be able to read the circuit and car and take a gamble on a complicated set of factors that include your own skills, your fearlessness or lack of it, and you wait, wait, wait, and then –

bosh – hammer the brake. And you do all of that in a fraction of a second.

Ideally, of course, you want to brake as late as you can, but the penalties are different. If you brake too early then you lose lap time, but that's preferable to braking too late, when you're probably going to drive off the circuit (see above). It's always a fine line between being brave enough or being too brave.

When a driver's trying to find the perfect spot to brake, they'll always work up to it through practice. The problem is that in practice you'll think you've found your perfect braking point, but by the time you get to qualifying two hours later, it's murder getting back in the zone to find it again.

Knit one, turn one

Your first braking point is the most important to get right for the whole lap. So, assuming everything's in working order and that your tyres are warmed up, you get to turn one, you've done the *wait, wait, wait* thing, you hammer the brakes and – *yes* – you've braked at the right point, you get the weight transfer, you turn in, feel that front grip, get to the apex, get back on the throttle and hey presto you've taken the corner perfectly, and that's your turn one, take a bow.

But if they threw that same corner at you five times, it's never going to be exactly the same five times over, because you're doing 200 miles an hour. You might think you're braking at the same point, but you'll always be a metre out, give or take.

In short, it's very, very tricky. And that first braking point is really what makes a lap – certainly a qualifying lap, because if you get that right, you're in a good place. Mentally, you're sorted, you know that the car is working as you want it to, and you approach turn two knowing that the car will do what you expect it to do: the tyre pressures are right, the brakes are at the temperature you need them to be, and the ride height is correct. Everything is working tickety-boo. And so, in theory, yes, everything should go smoothly after turn one. In theory.

This, of course, is a psychological trick as much as a genuine racing phenomenon, but it's true. After all, let's look at what happens in the other scenario: you get to turn one, brake too late and go wide, you've lost two-tenths of a second – at best, probably more than that – as a result of which then you start overdriving, because it's, like, *Right, I lost time, I need to drive harder than I was going to.*

Which is impossible. You're never going to catch up time because why would you have been driving slowly in the first place? But you do it anyway. You overdrive and then you brake too late, you lose grip, lock up and it gets worse. All because you made a dog's dinner of turn one.

In short, you need to get turn one right.

4. THE RACING LINE

The racing line is the quickest way through a corner, a means of taking the corner that fulfils the following criteria: a.) you're alive at the end of it; b.) your car is in one piece; and c.) you haven't lost any time, and may even have gained time over your rival. In other words, it's the shortest route around the corner and the route that lets you keep your minimum speed as high as possible.

My first-ever pole lap was Imola, 2004, in my BAR-Honda, and it's one of my most perfect-ever laps. Go find it on YouTube. I'll wait. I'll be talking about the noise it makes in due course, but for the time being watch how I'm using the kerbs, trying to get the most out of the kerb without going on the grass, which is where you start losing time. Watch the racing line, in other words.

I'm not going to be big-headed about this and say that it's a glorious symphony of braking, gear change and taking the ideal racing line. I'll just leave you to come to that conclusion yourself.

5. THE RULES OF OVERTAKING

You won't get very far in F1 if you have no heart for the overtake, which generally speaking will happen in a corner. If you have more power and you have more straight-line speed, you can overtake on the straight, but normally the finish of the move is done under braking and on a corner, which is where all that stuff I was banging on about earlier comes into play.

Turn one in Abu Dhabi, for example: you could get a good tow on the guy and then as it comes to the braking point, duck out, brake a little bit later and, as long as you place your car up the inside, pretty much the move is done.

But if you misjudge and he turns in, you've got to back out of it, which is tricky, because you're on the limit: there's a good chance you're going to lock up and run wide and maybe push him off the circuit as well. And you won't win many friends doing that. Then there's the risk that if you go in too deep and brake too late you'll go too far and he can get the switch back on and overtake you on the exit. What do you do?

Rule 1: Know your enemy

You need the guy you're overtaking to respect you, because a lot of the time you would dive down the inside, he'd turn in on you and you'd crash. He'll be hoping that you're going to back out and you'll be hoping that he's going to back out, so you end up crashing.

But just as you're trying to understand the driver, you don't want him to understand you. For example, if you try and make the move at a certain corner and it doesn't work, then he knows – or at least he thinks he knows – where you're going to try and overtake him next and he's going to block you; he'll come down the straight and if he thinks you're going to pull out, he'll just pull out and sit on the inside, so you can't get up in the inside of him for the corner.

Rule 2: Remember that there are actual rules, not just these made-up ones

The rule in a corner is that you're not allowed to brake and then move when you see someone trying to pass you, and the reason for that is because the guy behind has started braking also, and if he's trying to overtake you, he's on the limit of his braking power, so if you move in front of him, he's just going to drive over the top of you because he has no way of slowing down.

So that's banned. In theory. But on the first lap of the race, anything goes. Even though the FIA can see on the data when you've braked and penalise you for it afterwards, drivers think they'll get away with it because there's so much going on in that mental first lap of the race when everyone's adrenalin is so high.

Some will move by mistake, of course, just out of instinct. But all the drivers think and react differently, and there are certain drivers you know will not want to let you pass, even at the risk of crashing. Step forward Kevin Magnussen, who's known as a tough driver because he pushes the limits. So when you come up behind him to overtake, you want to make sure you've got the move done, otherwise you're going to crash.

Similar story on the straights, rule-wise. You can't move twice when someone's behind you. So, for example, if I try to overtake the guy in front, I'd go to the left and he would move to block me. He's allowed to do that, but he's not allowed to move back. It's just a rule to stop dangerous driving and make the racing better.

You always get guys who play fast and loose though. Tell you who was a demon on the corners: David Coulthard. He was, like, *Right, it's my corner, I'm going to turn in,* so I crashed with him a couple of times. He's a really tough guy to overtake because he wouldn't back out unless it was absolutely necessary. He'd just think, *Well, if you're alongside me, you've got the corner, but if you're not, you're going to have to back out* and he'd just turn in. Most of the time you couldn't back out, because you were on the limit.

Me, I was different. If the guy was coming up the inside, I'd be wary of him being unable to back out and so I'd give him room. It might not mean he's going to get the move done, but you won't turn in completely, you'll give him space. My thinking was that if I turned in we'd crash, but if I turned in a bit later and gave him room, we wouldn't crash, and I might still keep the position.

Rule 3: The inside is your friend

It's the shorter way around, of course, and you'll always try to go to the inside, but if you've tried it and failed and they've blocked you, you can give it a go on the outside, but more often than not you'll fail around the outside.

Often it will look as though the overtake is complete but the car being overtaken resumes its position in front, and that's because they've taken a shorter route through the corner. They've also been able to get on the power a bit earlier and they're more in control because they're in front, so they can push you off if they feel like it. Plus you're on the outside. You can't do anything. That's why you ideally need to stick to the inside for overtaking.

Rule 4: DRS is a drag

DRS is a 'drag reduction system' that operates a bit like a turbo boost when activated in certain DRS zones around the circuit. Overtaking with the DRS system has made it less exciting because drivers mostly overtake on the straight now because it's safer: you can use the DRS and power past.

If we didn't have it, we'd have to take more risks, which is the way it should be, I think. When I watch an Indy Car race around a circuit like Austin, it's great – so many overtaking moves and risky overtaking moves at that, because they don't have DRS. Overtaking is supposed to be really tough, but when you get a move done – a proper move, not a DRS move, a proper move – it's so rewarding. It's like standing on the podium. It's, like, *yes*. And if it's on your teammate it's even better. So, yes, boo hiss to DRS.

Rule 5: It's a shame when you're overtaken but you'll get over it

Sometimes you get caught napping. You're like, 'Oh, nuts, I should have seen that coming.' You thought he wasn't going to do it from that far back. Or you thought he was going to wait for the next corner.

But then it just happens, it comes out of nowhere. In NASCAR and Indy Car, you have a spotter. They'll communicate to the driver, 'He's on your inside, he's on your inside, he's coming up, he's just about to overtake!' But not in F1. It happens too quickly. It's, like, *bang*, done.

F1 is more exciting, though. It's because you know it's so difficult to overtake in F1 without DRS. So when you do make the move, it's shit hot, and if you make it on someone like Michael Schumacher back in the day, or Fernando Alonso, then it's really, really cool.

Still, we hate it, being overtaken. It's embarrassing. But then you've also got to think, *I'm racing against the best guys in the world, and if no one's going to overtake me, it's going to be a pretty boring race.* It's like a football player saying he's never going to be tackled. You've just got to take it on the chin.

Even so, it is definitely tough when you get overtaken, especially when they put a really good move on you, like they've braked late and they've caught you napping, as we say, leaving you wondering why you didn't cover the line, why you didn't block, why you gave him the opportunity to overtake.

That can be a bit embarrassing. Being overtaken from around the outside – as can sometimes happen in Austin – now that is *really* embarrassing.

Rule 6: Being irritating can pay dividends

It's not easy to overtake in any form of racing, but if you've fluffed it there's no point in thinking what might have been. You've got to get straight back on it, try and make the move again and try and do it immediately. You harass him, annoy him and he'll hopefully slip up, because he's already rattled and it happens that people brake too late, lock up and then you can pull things out of the fire and get the move done.

It's when you fluff a move and then you just sit behind the guy for the rest of the race – that's when it really hurts, probably worse than getting overtaken, actually, because you had an opportunity but you've failed at it and now you've got to spend the rest of the race sat behind this car that you should be pulling away from.

The last race of Super GT last year, I was in third, with the Championship contender behind. Whoever finished in front would win the Championship. He sat behind me for 20 laps trying to overtake but he didn't get past and that must hurt.

No kidding, my heart rate was through the roof knowing that if he got past me I'd destroyed the whole Championship for the team. He was probably faster, like a couple of tenths faster, but when you're in front that doesn't matter, especially when you're both dealing with traffic, as we were. I was taking fewer risks because I was the guy in front, whereas he was behind, risking everything because, why not?

Even crashing is better than finishing behind. We won, and it took me at least two days to get over the sheer adrenalin rush of that race.

Rule 7: You're at your most vulnerable when you've just done the overtaking (plus DRS is a drag, part 2)

You've made the move and you're past, but you've got a slightly worse exit because you've gone deep, and he regains the position. And I love it.

Those sorts of moves are great. The ones where you're battling the whole way. Fifty per cent of the time I'd say you get the overtake done and that's it, you never see them again, you just pull away and they're a fast receding dot in your mirrors.

But the other 50 per cent of the time? That's when it's game on and you get the proper dogfighting – and it's awesome.

This is another reason that the DRS is a drag. It's because it's got drivers judging where they make the overtaking manoeuvre. So say you have a hairpin followed by a straight, well, there's no point overtaking a car into the hairpin, because you exit and the car behind's going to get the DRS now – you can activate DRS as long as you're within one second of the car in front – so he's going to be able to pass you on the straight.

So, of course, you don't do that move, you wait until the straight and then you'll overtake him easily using your own DRS. It's reduced the excitement. It's taken away all that adrenalin of making a dive move, while the flipside is that when you're the one who's overtaken, you won't really care because you know the DRS zone's coming up and you can use that to get your place back. There's just less fight from both sides.

Rule 8: When you see your chance, take it

You could argue that racing is better in a formula that relies on mechanical grip rather than downforce, primarily because you don't lose mechanical grip when you're behind another car, whereas with downforce, you do.

No doubt the world of aerodynamics makes car design more interesting because it increases the top speed, but doesn't make the racing more interesting, it just makes it more difficult to overtake.

The reason is that you're in a car where the wings and floor are producing downforce. Now if you're behind a car, your floor won't really be affected – that will still be producing downforce – but the wings are. It feels like you've taken the wings off the car when you follow another car, which, as you might imagine, makes it more difficult to overtake. You go through a corner and the guy in front of you has full grip whereas you have lost 30 per cent of yours, meaning that when you turn in, you've got more front slide, more rear slide, less stability, and then the gap opens again.

That's why you have to know when to make your move – one of those skills that can't be taught – and you have to take it. If he's made a mistake, for example, you have to make your move, because as soon as he's gathered himself he's back to having more grip than you.

Your driving, meanwhile, will have to change to compensate for the fact that you've lost most of your grip, so if you roar into the corner right behind the car in front minus your front downforce, you have to pull out slightly and take a different line in order to try and recoup some of that lost grip from your wing.

So, for example, if it's a fast right-hander, you'll come down the straight and you'll pull out slightly so the air can hit the front of the wing. Otherwise you're going to turn in and find you have no front grip. In a low-speed corner, it's not so much of a problem. You pull out, you have all the downforce in the world, so if you pull out to overtake, you've got the same downforce as him.

And then you have the drag. So you've caught him up, and you're in his slipstream, meaning you're carrying more speed than him, and then under-braking, you wait for him to brake, you brake a fraction of a second later, you pull out, dive down the inside. It won't be the quickest line, but it doesn't matter, because once you're down the inside of him, he can't turn in.

You mess it up sometimes. You might go wide and go off the circuit. Or you'll lock up, because you've braked too hard, you get smoke, no grip as it slides and overheats. Plus a flat spot on your tyre which you'll have either for the rest of the race or until you pit for new tyres.

But there are other times that you don't mess it up. And those times are blissful. You've been setting up your manoeuvre from three or four corners before. You see what line the guy in front is taking and you're purposely trying to set him up and trying to get good tow up behind him so that you can dive down the inside, or down the outside, if he's blocking.

And then it's just… awesome.

Overtakes In Practice

Hungary, 2006, Me vs Schumacher

I overtook Michael into turn one, having started from the 14th. He didn't want to let me past, and there were some sweaty moments before he yielded, but ultimately I was able to sweep past.

Action with any driver's great, but with a legend like Michael – who at the time was driving a Ferrari – it's that bit more special. He was bloody tough but – with me, anyway – he was very fair. He never took the piss when it came to racing. He'd push you to the limit but he would never push you over it.

Like I say, I started at 14th and went on to win that race in the wet – my first win in Formula One – and that overtake was maybe the sweetest of the lot.

Canada, 2011, Me vs Vettel

Well, it was my greatest race, probably one of the greatest races in the history of the sport, and it was decided by this last-gasp overtake on Sebastian in the Red Bull. It wasn't a brilliant bit of overtaking from me: Sebastian was too focused on me in his mirrors and ran wide, and as long as I didn't do the same I was past him – and it probably wasn't as significant as the earlier lap in which I passed both Michael Schumacher and Mark Webber *in the same move* – but in the context of that particular four-hour race, not to mention the fact that it nicely bears out Rule 6 (*being irritating can pay dividends*), it was a doozy.

Hungary, 2012, Me vs Vettel

There are heaps of different types of moves. There are DRS moves, slingshots, braking manoeuvres... then there are those times when you get a superior corner exit, so you're getting a run on the car in front, and this one was a bit like that. Basically, I got better traction out of the previous corner. Why? Because it was a wet / dry race, we'd just put slicks on, I've got the tyres working better, saw a dry line and was able to get a good run on him out of the corner, putting his Red Bull squarely in my sights for the next corner. He saw me coming and tried to block but without as much conviction as he should have done, and I was on the inside, where it didn't matter if I braked a little too early.

Austin, 2012, Me vs Schumacher

Look at this overtake on YouTube and you'll see that most of the move is made on the straight here. I'm using his slipstream before pulling out and diving down the inside for the corner. This is Michael in a Mercedes, though, and he makes it very difficult for me.

Monaco, 2017, Me vs Hamilton

So this was my return and although it was only a practice session, according to commentators it was still ranked as one of the weekend's best overtakes. Lewis and I came out of the tunnel almost neck and neck, but I was the one who braked later going into the chicane, dived down inside of him, used the kerbs and came out just ahead. My last-ever overtake in Formula One, sniff.

6. VISIBILITY, POSITIONING

This is something that can differ quite considerably from car to car. I'm talking about the different years of car, but also different cars on the grid.

At McLaren in 2014 we went through a year where the visibility was poor. They had lifted the carbon cockpit from the steering wheel to the nose so they could get a better aerodynamic flow on the underside of the cockpit. As a result, the straight-ahead visibility wasn't too bad but the peripheral visibility was limited, so picking your turn-in point to a corner ended up being a bit of a guessing game.

I was, like, 'Guys, I can't see anything.'

'You can't see anything?'

'Not unless all you want me to see is the tyres, no.'

By that stage, of course, it was a bit too late to go back to the drawing board. Instead they just told me 'you'll get used to it', like it was just a prickly sweater, and not something that I had to drive at 200mph around Monaco.

I'm not sure that I ever did get used to it, though, and I don't think I was as precise in that car, purely because I had those visibility issues.

By Monaco I had asked for an extra piece of the seat to get me higher so I could see over the tyres, but then it just felt uncomfortable, as though I was sitting on top of the car. Ick.

So many of the issues around driver positioning are down to aerodynamics. The engineers are trying to design the car to where they think it's best for aerodynamics, and they tend to be afflicted by (wind) tunnel vision, so they forget about the driver a bit.

After that season we had a bit of a sit-down at McLaren – the drivers, the engineers and managers – and we drivers pointed out that any aerodynamic improvement was being cancelled out by the subsequent loss of confidence that comes from not being able to see.

Fair play, they were really good at listening to what the drivers had to say, and things changed so that we'd do the seat fitting at the factory before the tub was actually built; you'd sit in a mock-up, like a 3D-printed plastic thing identical to the proposed carbon-fibre tub, and they'd adjust things around you.

My biggest issue was inside the cockpit, because I'm taller than the average driver, the average being about five foot six, five foot eight, whereas I'm six foot. A little driver's fine, it's just about how much padding you have to put in the seat or in the car to make your seat up. A tall driver, you have to work bloody hard, days and days, to make sure that it fits correctly.

For instance, in the cockpit of the car you have a safety check. They pass a template around you to check that you're safe within the tub. For me, my legs were hitting the carbon fibre of the cockpit if I sat in my preferred position, so they had to move my bum back, which made me more upright, which was not a position I liked. It was a bloody nightmare. We got it right in the end and that was fine for a while. Oh, but then came the issue of where does all the stuff go? They had to put stuff in the car, like electronics boxes and wires, the fire extinguisher. And they installed all that but did that thing of forgetting about the driver again, until I said, 'Guys, I can't move my arms.'

They stood there scratching their arses, I mean chins. 'He can't move his arms. Does he need to move his arms? JB, do you need to move your arms?'

'Not really...'

'Well, that's great, then, problem solved.'

'...as long as I'm not called upon to corner at all, seeing as I can't steer.'

'But do you think that's how you drive?'

Deep breath. 'Yes, that's how I drive. It's not a train, it's a car.'

That convinced them, the train argument, and we came up with a compromise, where they left areas for my arms in which to move. I was a bit dubious at first, because there were still lumps and other obstructions that restricted my movement, but as it turned out they were right and once we'd jiggered things about a bit, I was mostly fine. I'd hit my elbow occasionally, of course – more than one car was guilty of being a real elbow hazard – I had to wear an elbow pad a lot of the time, and I found myself taking corners with my elbow in a weird position.

It was always funny how you'd find yourself driving around your position in the car. You'd spend the first part of the season getting used to it, the next few races thinking you'd cracked it, and then you'd go off for the break, come back again and find you'd lost all that residual muscle memory

I'd do exactly that and be like, 'Oh my God, what have you done? It feels *terrible*.'

And they'd go, 'We haven't done anything…'

Which meant I'd have to get used to it all over again.

Then you've got your wing mirrors. Key word there is vibration. As a result of which the other key words are. 'You can't' and 'see a bloody thing' – unless you count a distant blob as meaningful.

The thing is that if the wing mirrors are connected to the cockpit, it's not too bad, you can kind of see. And by 'kind of see' I mean that you're able to determine if there's someone behind you and whether he's going to the right or left, so that's fine for a while.

But then they went through a period where for aerodynamic reasons, teams were connecting the mirrors to the side pods. It was in response to a rule change in 2009, and all the teams did it. The first time they did that at McLaren, I pissed myself with laughter, because I could not see *a thing*. Like zero. Ground, sky, ground, sky, ground sky. It was just super, super high-frequency vibration. Reason being that the side pods aren't solid; they're carbon fibre, but they move, they shake around, they're just not designed to be as stiff as the cockpit.

As a result, there were accidents, of course, and I think a complaint was made to the FIA, which led to the FIA asking all the drivers, 'Are these mirrors okay?'

McLaren were like, 'We can't change it now and it's better for aerodynamics.'

So to the FIA I was like, 'Yes, they're fine,' and of course all the drivers swore blind that they could see perfectly, when in fact they couldn't see a thing.

Best of it was that the FIA would sit us in the car, stand behind us and say, 'Can you see me?'

No lying needed. 'Yup, I can see you perfectly.'

'How many fingers am I holding up?'

'That's not very polite, you're holding up two fingers, and not in the Winston Churchill way.'

(They love a joke, do the guys from the FIA.)

So anyway, it didn't take long for the FIA to cotton on to the fact that the teams were all telling porky pies, and the pod-mounted wing mirrors were banned in 2010. Good riddance.

7. THE SAFETY CAR

Safety cars are tricky. Obviously, the clue is in their name: they're a safety feature. But boy, do they have a tactical impact.

The idea of a safety car is that it appears during a 'caution period', either because there's stuff that needs clearing from the circuit, or because the weather's so shit that normal racing is dangerous.

The rules differ depending on the terms of deployment, but you're not allowed to pass the safety car or, more pertinently, each other, while it's out. The safety car, a Mercedes, will go at between

120mph and 150mph, which is pretty fast but still agonisingly slow compared to the speed of F1 cars, which should be going at over 200mph (top speed ever, by the way, is 231.5mph, recorded in a 2005 testing session by Juan Pablo Montoya in a McLaren-Mercedes), so what happens is that the field behind the safety car bunches up. Any lead you have? Wiped out. Were you trailing? Suddenly you're not. If you were the one who'd opened up a ten-second lead on the rest of the pack then it's a disaster. For the rest of the grid it's almost like resetting the race.

A lot of drivers use it as an opportunity to pit because you rejoin the race with new tyres or whatever and everybody's still going slowly. In Australia in 2015, I was coming around the second to last corner, saw that there was an accident, worked out that there would be a safety car and at the last minute was like, 'Guys, I'm going to pit, I'm going to pit,' and I threw the car to the right-hand side to get in the pit lane, only just missing a cone by the skin of my skinny-skin-skin, changed my tyres, got back out on the back of the safety-car train, and because I was in and out of the pits quickly other drivers when they pitted came out behind me.

As a result of that (rather quick-thinking if I do say so myself) manoeuvre, I was able to make up four places.

You don't have to pit, of course. Many do, and will adjust their strategy to accommodate the circumstance, but if it deviates too far from your chosen strategy you may simply decide not to. In this case, your job is to stay behind the safety car, fighting the loss of your tyre temperature, which you do by weaving and braking on the throttle, which puts heat into the disc and in turn, puts heat into the wheel which puts heat into the tyre.

It's something we do before starts as well, a tactic we've learnt to do over the years. We did lots of different tests with our tyre guys. The best way of braking in order to put core temperature into the tyres was to hammer the brakes. Bang, bang, bang, really quickly.

Lastly, let's spare a thought for the poor sod leading, because if you're out in front, a safety car is the worst thing ever. You hate it with a passion, it's horrible. Not only does the gap close, but the chances are you will have been on a completely different strategy. So you might be on tyres that are much older than the car in second – he's on a two-stop strategy, you're on a one-stop strategy – you might even have had a 30-second lead on him, but he's just pitted, come out with new tyres, he's 30 seconds behind, and then a safety car comes so the gap closes up and he's now right behind you on brand-new tyres and you're screwed, basically.

8. PIT STOPS, FUEL, ETC.

Shanghai, 2011. In testing, we at McLaren had performed practice pit stops, as was usual. The only thing was that in practice the crew had been wearing black, but for the race itself they had changed into silver suits.

I knew that they'd changed, of course. It's not like they crept off in secret to do it – an amusing trick to play on Jenson. But the fact that they had changed suits had momentarily slipped my mind, what with me being busy driving eight million dollars' worth of car at over 200mph, leading the race with Sebastian's Red Bull in second, and then being called in to pit, slowing down to the pit limit of 50mph under considerable G and braking for the line, and… Pulled up short into Sebastian's box, which was first along the pit lane, because Red Bull had won the Championship the previous year.

Worse still, Sebastian was trying to pit behind me. All credit to Red Bull, they saw what I'd done, reacted quickly and waved me through into the right pit box.

Believe me, it is easily done. Like I say, you're braking, you're looking up for the pit box, expecting to see a certain colour, and you don't realise that the reason they're standing there with a trolley ready and waving at you is not actually for you but for Sebastian behind – and so you pull up.

But I was mortified, and no doubt very unpopular with Sebastian and Red Bull as a result. To make up for it I shall now provide them with a free advertisement. *Red Bull… gives you wings.*

Mind you, any popularity with Sebastian and Red Bull was temporary. Because of what we shall now call the Pit Stop Bollock Drop, he was able to get out of the pits first. Next thing you know, Lewis pitted on the next lap, selected the correct pit box and got out in front of me as well. So I was third.

All in all, it was a little bit frustrating and embarrassing – more embarrassing than anything else. Some bloke even did a 'should have gone to Specsavers' parody on YouTube.

Why do you pit? Because you need a new wing or new tyres, or a change of tyres because of degradation. That could be because you want to use wet or dry or try a different composition. I should mention the little doohickeys they have to tell whether you've got enough tread on the tyre to last the race. They can monitor to see if you're going to get through to the canvas of the tyre, which is the underpinning of the tyre, before the end of your stint, and be like, *Hang on, you've got to take it easier on that tyre, because you're going to destroy it.*

Hopefully, it won't ever get that far, of course, because when it gets to the canvas, you have no grip whatsoever and as a safety precaution Pirelli will say no, you've got to pit.

For most of my career, you might also be pitting for fuel, which is one of those things that has required various different strategies throughout the years.

Some people would start with a full tank, 100kg of fuel; some would start with 50kg of fuel, which on the one hand made you much quicker, but on the other meant that you were going to have to pit earlier and maybe more frequently.

It was one of those great things that you could do to make your race fun or if you found yourself starting in tenth. Like, you could make it more interesting by doing a one-stop race when you knew that other people were doing a two-stop because nobody wanted to start with full tanks, but you risked it because the one-stop works and if you're starting in tenth then what do you have to lose? Apart from making a fuel of yourself. (See what I did there?)

There was also a period where you had to use any fuel you had in the car. You filled up, did your qualifying and then afterwards everyone found out how many laps of fuel you had left for the race itself, a bit like pinning test results on the board at school.

So let's say if you did qualifying with 40kg left in the tank, that's what you'd start the race with. So if you qualified on pole with 40kg but the guy behind you had qualified with 60kg, it'd be all, 'Uh oh,' because that would be an extra ten laps he could do on his fuel. You'd be quicker to start the race, but he might have to stop less than you.

That was really good. I really enjoyed that type of racing, it was fun doing qualifying, which was great anyway, and then afterwards you'd be waiting for the results to come in, saying, 'Oh, bollocks', because your rival's got five more laps' worth of fuel than you. We'd base our strategies around it. We'd have to coincide refuelling with tyre changes, so if we knew that our tyres would be destroyed after ten laps, you only put ten laps of fuel in.

Now, they don't stop at all for fuel. Mid-race refuelling was banned for good in 2010 as a safety precaution, which is a bit of shame – Google 'Kimi Räikkönen pit-stop fire 2009' for at least part of the reason why. Basically, you just change tyres during a pit stop, which is a bit boring in my book. How many times we stop depends, but normally it's the same for teammates. So if, for example, Mercedes get off the line in Barcelona, and they're one–two, the guy in second is probably going to finish second, because he's not going to be able to overtake his teammate by using a different strategy – he won't be allowed, which takes away strategy and excitement. And, of course, if the two drivers do end up on different strategies, then there are ructions.

Case in point: Barcelona, 2009, the Spanish Grand Prix. I went off the line, but was overtaken by Rubens, my teammate. At the beginning of the race we were both on a three-stop strategy because that, according to the strategists, was the best, quickest strategy, but having been overtaken by my teammate, I was in the mood to try something different and got on the radio to the team.

'Okay,' they said, 'ditch the three-stop strategy, we'll let you try two. You'll be slower, because you'll be heavier, but you won't have to stop three times, you'll just stop twice. The strategists say you'll still finish second.'

'I want to take the risk,' I said.

The idea was that instead of getting 50kg, I'd get 90kg. 'Look after the tyres,' they advised, 'be consistent, keep up your lap times, see what you can do.'

And I did, and I ended up winning by 13 seconds. Fortune, as they say, favours the brave and it was a risk – a gamble that relied on me being able to keep up fast lap times and on Rubens perhaps slowing down a little.

Afterwards, however, Rubens was a little miffed. He'd been with Ferrari when Ferrari had unabashedly given Michael Schumacher number one status and was making all sorts of noises about jumping ship if a similar situation arose again. Who could blame him? Any suspicion that there were team orders in play must surely have been put to rest by the fact that he got past me in the first place, though.

These days you can start with a maximum of 100kg of fuel. But say you run 90kg of fuel, you're going to be quicker, because 10kg of fuel is worth three-tenths per lap. In other words, if you're able to run only 90kg in the race instead of 100kg, every lap will be three-tenths quicker.

So that's good on the one hand. But then you have to play the percentages. You'll need to save fuel by braking early and lifting off for some corners, and hope that it adds up to enough that you've got sufficient fuel for the end of the race.

When I won Suzuka in 2011, I had basically run out of fuel. I had two laps to go and they said, 'You're not going to make it, you're not going to make it, you have to lift everywhere.'

At this stage I had a ten-second lead, but now I was having to go easy on brakes and throttle in order to conserve fuel, being super-aware that behind me Fernando in a Ferrari was closing the gap.

Sweating.

Arse cheeks clenched as tight as my teeth.

And I crossed the line in first with a half-second lead and immediately ran out of fuel.

Mind you, the team don't come right out and tell you how you've got to handle your fuel. We're well aware that people are listening in, so they use code, so it's like 'Fuel One', 'Fuel Two', 'Fuel Three', and so on.

'Fuel One' would be, *You have to brake 20 metres later at turn one, turn seven and turn 12*.

'Fuel Two' would be, *You have to brake 20 metres later at turn one, five, seven, nine and thirteen*, and then 'Fuel Three' would be, *You've got to lift off 50 metres for every corner*.

And because you're saving fuel, you're also looking after the tyres and the brakes, so sometimes you don't actually go much slower. It's judging what's better for overall lap time, what's better for overall race distance.

Funnily enough, I actually enjoyed that part of it. The problem was that the Honda engine was a bit thirsty, so we would use more fuel than other people. So sometimes we'd fill the tank up completely and still would have to save fuel every lap.

I remember at Melbourne 2015, the first year we used a Honda engine at McLaren, I was working so hard to conserve fuel that I ended up finishing two laps down. I was braking so far ahead of the 100-metre braking board that I was just floating into corners. It's a weird feeling.

Incidentally, if you did a double-take at the thought of other teams listening in to our talkback, then I've got news for you: it happens all the time. Of course, the broadcasters are able to listen to all of the teams' radio chatter all of the time, if they so please, but so can the teams. (Or, I should say, they certainly used to – because I'm sure it doesn't happen now.)

It was awesome – you'd hear all the secret stuff. They brought in people who could hack the radios, but nobody seemed to mind because we were all doing it; it was like an open secret in the sport.

Same with the spies. All the teams would have cameramen walking down the pit lane pretending to be fans and getting pictures in the garage of the new parts of the car and things like that.

These guys would stand, like, 50 metres away and still be able to get pictures that looked as though they were standing right next to the car. We used to have people looking out for them, who would then stand in their way. They soon worked out who were the genuine fans and who were the spies.

I remember a time with Brawn when we were debuting a new car, and we'd pull the garage shutters down, put screens up. Some of the photographers were pretty shameless, they'd just dangle their camera over the top of the screens and click away in the (usually vain) hope of catching something useful. At some of the circuits – Barcelona, for example – they have balconies above the garage and so the photographer would station themselves on those, lean over and snap away.

They'd pretend to be press photographers, of course. After a while the whole practice got a bit out of hand, and so the teams and the media came to an understanding that any pictures would have to include personnel. So what you had then was the driver standing in front of the car, arms folded, doing his driver pose, cameraman clicking away.

And then you'd see the camera lens move a little as the cameramen tried to get whatever part he'd been asked to focus on. And the driver would see, and he'd subtly alter his position to cover up the interesting part. So the cameraman, under the guise of trying to get a fresh angle or a different shot would crouch and move, and the driver would shift again, and the whole time they've both got these fixed grins, going through the motions. It was hilarious.

Which brings us back to pit stops. In NASCAR they have specific pit-stop guys, whereas in F1 the mechanics who are working night and day on the cars are also doing the pit stops. It's amazing and it's become quite a competition between teams. You get the fastest pit-stop award: two seconds to change four tyres.

Things are different again in Super GT, where we come in, they plug in and the car goes up on its own, raised by internal jacks.

So in F1 you've got the lollipop there, which stops you, or lights, and then the car goes up on the jack thanks to the trolley man, plus the tyres are heavier and difficult to manoeuvre, and they're still doing two-second pit stops. It's staggering. It really does put the team in the formula, because it's the one time that we as drivers are very literally bystanders, or bysitters, if you want to be pedantic about it. These guys have to stand in the pit lane with a car hurtling towards them and then do the job in two seconds flat, running the risk of being lampooned as a bunch of hapless slow-coaches if they take any longer than that.

Meanwhile, as drivers all we have to do is stop in the right pit box – and like I say, we don't always get that right.

9. WEATHER

I've already sung the praises of the garage crew, so let's hear it for some more of the unsung heroes of Formula One: the strategists. Whatever these guys get paid they're worth more, because it's a tough job and all they get is shit for it.

What do they do? Good question. Dunno. Okay, I do. What they do is run different scenarios and base strategies upon it and from these they'll form a race strategy that they present to you, the driver, and your race engineer.

Typically, you'll have two strategists at the circuit and then a load more back at base, and between them they run the race something like 800 times, conjuring differing race strategies based on each scenario: what would happen if you pitted on Lap 14, if you pitted on Lap 20, if you pitted on Lap 25? What would happen if you had this much more pace compared to the cars around you, or they were this much quicker than you? Where would you finish?

No kidding, the sheer volume of differing possibilities they run through is unreal. What you'll do, how you'll do it, whether or not an escaped giraffe will maraud through the paddock. You're in awe.

'Right, JB,' they'll announce eagerly, as though about to give you the greatest gift in the world, 'if the race runs smoothly and you have the pace we expect you to have, you're going to finish… eighth.'

And you're like, 'Great. Eighth. That's… great.'

Or else they'll say, 'We've run the race a zillion times and you should win by ten seconds, easy,' and you gulp because the pressure's on but at least you have a chance of winning, before they add, 'But that's if everything goes to plan, because if X happens, you won't win.' The idea being that they're ready for anything, every possible scenario.

This is all 'in theory', of course, because as we all know – and in fairness, so do the poor old strategists, whose entire existence is one long procession of thwarted outcomes and unexpected resolutions – life has a pesky way of not sticking to the script. Things never turn out the way you expect, because nothing ever goes to plan. As a strategist you can legislate for your own driver (and even then…) but not for all the other drivers on the grid.

And what they also find most difficult to predict, of course, is the weather. Like all of us they're looking at the weather forecast, and like the rest of us they're wondering if it's going to do what it's supposed to do.

In certain circuits it rains from only one direction, which is quite weird. Fuji, if you see the clouds over the volcano Mount

Fuji, and they're dark clouds, you know it's going to rain in a certain amount of time, which is quite funny. All the Japanese know that, nobody else does.

Other races, if it's cloudy in a certain area, you know it's going to rain. Spa's like that, too. The teams station guys at turn five, all the way down the back straight, which is about 2.5kms away from the pit lane and garages, and they stand there just to keep an eye on the weather, because that's the direction the weather will come from, and if they say it's starting to rain, then you know it's going to be coming down properly in ten minutes.

Tell you this much, though, one way of knowing that you're at a Grand Prix, apart from the noise, the stands, the sponsorship, is that a lot of people in branded polo shirts will be looking up at the sky.

Myth: People think I prefer it in the wet.
Truth: Even though, I'm probably better in the wet I still prefer it to be dry.

I think the fact is that I just deal with the wet better than others. Apart from my second-to-last race in 2016, which I'll come to, I get excited when it starts raining because I know that we can mess around with the strategy and try different things.

The other extreme is unbelievably hot like, unbelievably hot, melting the tyres almost. Those are tough races, Bahrain is always very hot. But perhaps the hottest I ever recall was one time in Germany. It was 40 degrees. Celsius.

As drivers we were having freezing cold water poured on the veins of our arms (pro tip: cold water on the veins cools you down); we were wearing cool vests; we were keeping our heads wetter than a baptised baby's; we were drinking lots and staying hydrated; we had people holding umbrellas over our heads, wafting little handheld fans at us and singing songs of glaciers and polar bears; we had literally *the whole team* focused on keeping us cool.

And the poor grid girls were dropping like flies in the heat.

As for the race, it makes it very different, because you really have to be careful with the tyres. Most of the time your problem is keeping the heat in your tyres but in heat like that the opposite is true because they overheat very quickly, and while you might think that a hot tyre being a sticky tyre equals A Good Thing, it's not if gets too hot and it blisters, then you get chunks of it flying off, you're sliding everywhere and you'd have to pit for new tyres. That particular race in Germany ended up being a four-stop race for most of us.

In the heat you'll move towards the harder of the tyres that you're allowed to use, because they blister less and are better in the heat. We test different tyres at different temperature ranges, so we know that such and such a tyre will work in 25 degrees circuit temp, this one's 40 degrees circuit temp. Even though it may be the same compound, it will work differently with different temperatures.

Then there are races that are cool, and the opposite is true: you're struggling to get tyre temperature.

The worst thing in a cool race is that you'll be 15 laps into a stint with worn tyres – a 'stint' being the period of time you spend on a set of tyres – and then you get a safety car going slowly. At Spa, it's often cold, but the thing with Spa is that you've got a lot of high-speed corners, so you can get heat into the tyres. It's the circuits that don't have the high-speed corners that are more tricky. Other cold circuits? Australia can be cold. Silverstone, Austria. A beautiful circuit, it's stunning, the Austrian race. A tiny little circuit, but beautiful surroundings, it's really pretty, very green. But it's very cold.

Plus it's full of Red Bull fans.

BIG TRUCKS

So this all began with my best mate Chrissy Buncombe's 40th birthday looming and me scratching my head, trying to think what to get him.

I had no idea until I spoke to another mate who said, 'What about doing something, like, in a car? You know, considering that Chrissy is a racing driver as well...'

Which was like, *Whoa*. The answer was there right in front of me.

We're going to do Baja.

Baja 1000 is a desert race held at the Baja California Peninsula every November. At 1,000 miles long, it's the longest off-road race in the world. Various types of vehicle classes compete on the same course with classes for cars, trucks, motorcycles, ATVs and buggies. It's like a cross between *Wacky Races* and *Mad Max*.

And it's So. Bloody. Cool.

So that was it – happy birthday, mate, we're going to do Baja, my treat, and the idea was that we'd rent a buggy, the lowest category, and one of us would drive, one would co-drive, that was the idea. So, his birthday, I told him, he was made up about it, and I was, like, *Right, I'm going to go down to check out where they make these trucks.* Brenthel Industries, in California, a nice, two-hour pootle down the coast. Got there and walked in, seeing big off-road trucks, thinking, *Oh my God, these things are mega,* getting a bit excited now, feeling the project shift from 'nice idea' to actual pistons and metal.

I said to the owner guy, Jonathan Brenthel who runs it with his brother, Jordan, 'Do you do buggies?'

'Yeah,' he said, 'we do – we do this off-road thing, it's called a Class One. It's like 600 horsepower though, it's not like the bottom category.'

'How much is that to rent?'

'For Baja?'

'Yeah, for Baja.'

'That would be a hundred grand.'

I swallowed something hard and jagged. I said, 'A hundred grand. That's quite a lot of money, isn't it?'

'Yes,' he said, and went on to explain that 'you need a week of practice and you have to run through all the systems, and then there's the race itself. If you have a bad day it could take you up to thirty-five hours.'

'Thirty-five hours?'

'Well, yeah, you're not doing a hundred miles an hour the whole way. You're off-road. Some sections are twelve miles an hour.'

There are actually two courses for Baja: the point-to-point, which is about 900 miles, for which the current best time is just over 21 hours, and 'the loop', which is fewer miles, and has been done in just over 16 hours.

I was, like, 'Okay, so what about these trucks here? These off-road trucks? How much are they to rent?'

'They're a hundred grand.'

I'm starting to wonder about his pricing system. Is everything a hundred grand here? *This is a lot of money,* my earlier excitement replaced by wondering if I should have just got Chrissy a *Fast & Furious* boxset. 'Okay. Then how much to buy one?'

He said, 'Well you can buy it for $190,000 and I've got one for sale with two engines, 450 horsepower, 550 horsepower, brand new.'

Now, sure, I'm the one who bought not one but two yachts. But even to me that sounded better business sense than renting one for the day, even with the costs of running it for the Baja because you don't just buy the car, you need a team to run it for refuelling, tyre changes and all that.

'I'll take one,' I said.

Chrissy came over for testing and we went out into the desert. At this stage it was just a tubular frame with no body and it looked like a proper *Mad Max* car, the scariest-looking thing you've ever seen.

I jumped in with Jordan, me in the driver's seat, him in the passenger seat. It's an upright seat, really elevated. I was going over bumps that were six, seven feet high, and it felt awful. I was only doing 35 miles an hour and the truck was going all over the place, and I was yelling, 'Is this good? Is this all right?' at Jordan, because it sure as hell doesn't feel good or all right.

'It's all right,' he tried to reassure me, until we'd done the whole loop, at which point he took a deep breath like at last the torture was over, and said, 'Right, I'm going to take you for a drive now.'

I shook my head. 'I'm not very good as a passenger, I never get in as a passenger.'

He said, 'No, you need to let me drive. You need to see what this truck can really do.'

So I thought, *Okay. Right.* Swapped places. And we went to the same section and I'm not kidding, he took the bumps at 90mph.

'Look what it can do,' he bawled as we raced headlong towards towering dunes. I'm like, *brace, brace, brace,* but then – boom – it was like climbing a staircase; this thing was literally floating over the dunes.

'I'm flat, I'm flat, I'm flat, I'm flat,' he was shouting as we reached top speed, and still the truck was eating up these dunes. What happens is that when you go at speed, the truck never falls into the bumps, so it just floats across the top. It feels counter-intuitive, like driving with downforce. With downforce you have to get your head around the fact that the quicker you go, the more downforce you generate, the more grip you have. It's exactly the

My very first
motorhome, a thing
of intense beauty.
Note the leopard-
skin interior theme
and sink *right* next to
the bed. A paradise.

(© Mercury Press)

Little Missy, my boat,
which put me in
debt. Good times.

(© Motorsport Images)

Don't call it a comeback. Monaco 2017 on one of my favourite circuits. Site of my very last overtake in Formula 1, against Lewis Hamilton. This is the MCL32 on track during qualifying. (© Thompson/Staff/Getty)

This is BAR-Honda driver Anthony Davidson in 2004 at Monza, in a car that perfectly shows what it's like to sit, or lie, in an F1 car. (© DPA Picture Alliance/Alamy Stock Photo)

Sitting pretty in Brazil in 2009 with the rest of team Brawn, complete with terrifying head covering before the helmet-hat goes on.

(© Thompson/Staff/Getty)

Mister Freeze. This is the McLaren team preparing me for a practice drive in Singapore, 2010.

(© Hoch Zwei/Contributor/Getty)

For a tall driver, things can get cramped – *Me:* 'I can't move my arms.' *Mechanics:* 'Do you need to?' *Me:* 'No, not really... as long as I don't need to corner...'

(© Darren Heath)

Taking on the Mint 400, the gruelling off-road race in the middle of the Nevada desert. 130 miles, *Mad Max* style! (© Eric Simpson Photography)

Driving Le Mans is like having five tequilas before lunchtime. Here I am *trying* and somewhat failing to get out of the car in 2018. (© Jean-Francois Monier/Contributor/Getty)

Mirror, signal, manoeuvre... Oh shoot! When a crash happens, you're devastated. Not for yourself, understand, but for your mechanics, who are now probably facing an all-nighter to put the whole thing back together again. Sorry guys. (© Associated Press)

The intense weather in Brazil 2016. Wet conditions are usually perfect for me, but this was one of the few times I ever got The Fear in an F1 car. (© Motorsport Images)

The thing about F1 is that you're sort of, not really, but kind of definitely, always at war with your teammate. So, it was particularly kind of Rubens to design me this t-shirt... (© Motorsport Images)

Simulators: it's a love-hate relationship. On the hate side, they're rarely accurate enough to be of much use, and the motion sickness can lead to vomit. On the upside, um, well, who doesn't love a bit of *Mario Kart*? (© Roslan Rahman/Staff/Getty)

Another Oscar-worthy performance in *Tooned*, with Lewis Hamilton, and chatting on the podium after the Grand Prix in Silverstone, in 2017. (above © McLaren, right © AFP Contributor/Contributor/Getty)

Below: The look of love. (© Motorsport Images)

This is how you do it – thumb right over the end when you shake, then release a tiny bit to spray. Pick out your targets and angle carefully. Melbourne, 2010, winning the Australian Grand Prix.

(© Mark Thompson/Staff/Getty)

Always have a signature celebration ready. No.1. in Monaco, 2009.

(© Paul Gilham/Staff/Getty)

same downright wonky thinking at work here. The faster you go in this truck, the more capable it is over the desert terrain.

'Now we're going to go across some squarer bumps where you have to slow down,' yelled Jordan.

'You what? It looks exactly the same,' I replied. 'How do you know that's a square, not a rounded-off bump?'

He said, 'You'll get used to it, it's the angle and the colour of the sand.'

I said, 'It's all the same colour, isn't it? It's yellow.'

'You'll get used to it,' he assured me.

But I drove again and I was so lost. It was the most fish-out-of-water I'd ever been.

Chrissy was the same. We were both, like, *This is batshit crazy driving.* We were testing that truck like we've never raced anything in our lives, but also enjoying it in a weird way and then we did more laps, more times, a couple more days, it was, like, we love it, it's the best thing we've ever done. Why? Because we're both racing drivers and as I've already pointed out, racing drivers love to learn. Learning something, pushing it to the limit. That's what really turns us on.

So we did a race earlier this year, the Mint 400, and we did 130 miles each.

Chrissy did it first, and we were pretty pleased, thinking we'd got the hang of the truck, until we looked at the times and discovered that we'd qualified last, one-and-half minutes off the pace. This on a five-minute course.

He was like, 'I don't get it. I feel like I've lost all my racing skills. It's just so different.'

Not to be deterred we set off on the race itself, and after two hours each of driving it in the desert, we loved it and we were actually doing pretty well. In terms of speed, the trucks are very quick. They can do 145mph on dirt, which is seriously quick for that kind of surface, plus you feel like you're doing twice the speed you are. It's like driving a speedboat, basically.

We worked out that you've got to relax, because if you tense up, you're going to roll it. One of our guys did that. He hit a bump wrong during his stint, rolled it, it landed on its wheels, he got it back to the pits, they welded some things up, and we carried on – all in the dark.

We ended up finishing 19th out of 45 in our category. Not too bad, all told, and it certainly left us looking forward to Baja, which looks like being absolutely wild (it is, at the time of writing, yet to happen). After all, it's proper lawless, *Mad Max* tackle. You drive through housing estates and along dried-up riverbeds. Spectators stand dangerously close (and are constantly getting mown down if the YouTube videos I've seen are anything to go by).

A lot of trucks get stuck in the sand, because it's really silty and these things are proper heavy. Sometimes you get eight or nine trucks stuck because the first truck got wedged in the sand the rest have had to stop and got stuck themselves.

In the Mint 400 there are fuel stops and we'd stop to swap drivers, but at Baja we don't stop for eight hours. For eating we have nutrition bars and gels that you squirt in your mouth. Although most people who race there don't eat properly, we're determined that we will, because it makes a massive difference, especially when you're driving at night. You need focus.

As for going to the loo, you have to wear a catheter on your willy and piss in the truck so it goes down your trouser leg and comes out the bottom. It's like being in *The Flintstones*.

And I suppose that secretly (and even not-so secretly) I love all that. It's old-school, grass-roots racing. I mean, you go up through the categories in motor racing and they get so much more serious as you go up from Formula Four to Formula Three, and then to Formula One. It's super serious when you get to the top and if you're not super serious with it then you're out on your ear, and rightly so.

But even so, you look back at those old karting days and think what great fun it all was.

And of course there's no pressure. I don't go in as Jenson Button, Formula One champ, I go along as Jenson Button, just another bloke. To be honest, not many people in the US even know who I am. Like when I first went to the Brenthel brothers, Jordan said to me, 'Do you have any experience?"

I looked at him and smiled, because I thought he was taking the piss. He wasn't. 'Yeah,' I said, I've been circuit racing for many years, racing Formula One for seventeen years.'

He said, 'Oh, that's so cool.'

He didn't really know what Formula One was. And then on

the way home, he texted me saying, 'JB, that F1 stuff is so rad,' (Californian, see), and ever since I've been taking the piss out of him for being in the motorsport business but not knowing what Formula One is.

And that's been the way with all the people that are partnering with us. Most of them have no idea about Formula One, which is great because it's a very level playing field, and helps build a real team atmosphere, which is something I definitely miss from motorsport. Super GT has that, but this is another level of chilled – guys who have the opportunity to go racing in trucks. It's really cool and a great challenge. Something new to learn.

THE SWAG

1. THE ENGINES AND THE LOVELY NOISE
THEY MAKE

Remember that Imola pole lap? How I said we'd be talking about the noise it made? Well, this is the bit where I talk about the noise it made.

Okay. First thing to note: It's a V10, and I love V10s. I like V8s less and I really dislike V6s.

V10s, though. Whoosh. The noise that a V10 makes is unreal: high-pitched yet dangerous; full-throated and insistent. And if you think it sounds good on your phone's speaker, imagine being in the cockpit. Even with earplugs fitted the noise is awesome, and I mean that literally. It takes your breath away. It envelops you – it puts you at the centre of the machine's industry; it reminds you that you're not so much the driver of this incredible piece of machinery as a mere component of it.

Nowadays, of course, they use more powerful engines than that. What I drove then was probably 850, maybe 860 horsepower, whereas now they're over 900 horsepower. Even so, they're a V6 engine compared to a three-litre, and they just don't sound the same.

Nor do they feel the same. The V6 1.6 is turbocharged and has the electronic recovery system, which gives it 160 horsepower of electric power. When I was in Barcelona for Sky TV we compared my Barcelona Brawn pole-position lap – which was in a V8 – with Valtteri Bottas's pole position in a 1.6 litre V6 at the same circuit. From the line to turn one, which isn't that far, he had pulled about 10 metres on me just in the tiny little straight, because of how much more power he had.

On the approach and then through the corners, our respective speeds were similar. But then as soon as he accelerated out of the corner, he gained speed – simply because that's the way it works with the electric power and turbo-charger. They're faster.

So fast equals good, yes? True. But – and it's big but for a driver – they're not as nice and not nearly as much fun to drive. Whereas in the V10 and V8 era, you'd get on the throttle, sense the power coming in more gradually on the corner exits and feel at one with the car, knowing that you were absolutely in control of it, now it's just *bang*, there's power there, but you don't feel like the one in charge.

Overall, though, and speaking more as a fan and pundit than as a driver, it's the noise I miss most. Moving from V10 to V8 was a bit of a wrench, because they didn't sound quite as good, and that carried us through from 2006 to 2013 – and then 2014 was the new hybrid era, which we're still in, and I remember everyone was, like, 'Oh my God, what have they done?' Because the whole thing about F1 was the feeling of being about a mile away from the circuit and hearing the cars going round. It was beautiful. And if you had guests at a race weekend, you took them to the garage, and watched their reaction as soon as the car was started. They'd be like, 'Oh my God,' big grins all over their faces.

I understand the reasons why – don't get me wrong, I'm an enthusiastic recycler, and I think it's quite possible to simultaneously miss something and yet approve of its passing – but the fact is that it's just not quite the same. I mean, I'm sure Mercedes are happy because they've won almost every race with the hybrid engines, but it's just not that beautiful noise it used to be.

It's the same right across the board. These days supercars now have a little speaker in them to make them sound more supercar-ish, but to me it just sounds fake.

Then you've got Formula E, where everything is electric. So obviously the cars aren't very loud, but it's a massive championship and all the manufacturers want to be involved because it's the testing ground for what will soon be the dominant technology.

And that's all good. But I still kind of wish that we could let Formula One have its beautiful-sounding engines.

2. MECHANICAL GRIP VS DOWNFORCE

So we all know what downforce is, yes? It's grip, but grip that is generated via the aerodynamics of the car, whereas mechanical grip is what we have on our road cars – grip that is generated chiefly by the tyres.

I don't know if it's true of all racing drivers, but personally I feel like I have a complicated relationship with downforce, and perhaps now is the time to try and make sense of it on paper.

Firstly, I always felt in the past that it's better to have mechanical grip because you know what you're getting. I believed that it was simpler for everyone to understand, and that you can race more excitingly with mechanical grip, which allows proper wheel-to-wheel racing in a way that downforce does not.

After all, when you picture cars racing, you see images from films and TV or old-school motorsport: cars jockeying for position, drivers wrestling with the wheel, a scrappy synthesis of man and machine. The contemporary Formula One model, where cars make use of aerodynamics to sweep imperiously past one another, is anathema to all of that. To the uninitiated it looks like one car simply passes the other, and it can be difficult to understand why that has happened.

But that's what I see with these rose-tinted spectacles I'm currently wearing. And having now raced in Super GT where mechanical grip is more powerful than the downforce, I actually find it tougher to understand what the car is doing. I find it much more difficult to do what I need to do to improve the balance of the car.

For that reason I struggle when it comes to setting up the Super GT car and really pushing it to the limit, whereas if we had lots of downforce, well, I know how that works. After 17 years I'm used to it.

And I really never thought I'd hear myself say that, because I *always* thought mechanical grip was better.

I first encountered downforce in Formula Three, having come from karting, which was mechanical grip, pure and simple, and I struggled at first. Moving on to F1 was good, to begin with, because the car I drove – the Williams FW22 – was such an easy car to drive. So easy, in fact, that I didn't really put a lot of effort into learning about aerodynamics. It was only when I suddenly had a difficult car to drive – the Benetton B201 – and I really had to work on it. So yes, they did need to sit me down and teach me about aerodynamics and the best way to get lap time out of aero-dynamics and it's really important. It sounds silly but I remember thinking, *Oh my God, why didn't you tell me this earlier?* It's some-thing you really have to learn because it seems so unnatural.

I can't really advise on how to drive a car with lots of down-force. You need to get in one, which you probably won't be able to do until you've mastered the mechanical grip of another category. It's one of those weird catch-22 situations.

3. THE DREADED SIMULATOR

I've got a confession to make. Last year I bought a PlayStation. That's not the confession. That's just setting the scene for the confession.

I hadn't had a games console for going on 20 years, but I bought it because I'd entered the Le Mans 24-Hour Race (more of which later) and I was due to go there and test. The idea is that you test for one weekend before racing the following weekend, and the fact that there are three guys in the team means you get hardly any circuit time – between eight and ten laps only – so I thought it'd be a good idea to take a Le Mans crash course via the wonders of video game technology.

So anyway. I expected to just switch on the computer, or console, or whatever they call it, and play like we used to do in the old days, when games came on a cartridge not a disc or a download, and you whiled away entire summer holidays playing *Super Mario Kart*, drinking tins of Fanta and burping the theme tune to *Jaws*.

But this thing took bloody ages to load, or upload, or download, or update, or whatever the hell it was doing. And then when I did eventually get to play it became apparent that I had to play it for 250 hours just to reach the Le Mans section of the game.

So the PlayStation was packed away, and instead I phoned up my mate down the road. This bloke has built a simulator in his living room. I mean it – you wouldn't believe the amount of effort that's gone into it. No word of a lie, you walk into his normal-sized living room, with its sofa, two chairs and a desk, and it all looks normal except for the fact that on the other side of the room is this sit-in simulator, with a shell that lifts up, and inside that a seat – a proper racing-car seat that you strap yourself into – and a 2D surround screen. You've also got a pedal box for your feet, all of which is properly sprung and dampened, a proper steering wheel that will give you feedback.

I think it's still all played through a PlayStation, so it is in effect a glorified game console, but it's a completely different beast from what I'd packed away at home. The quality and feel of it was just unreal – or should that be the other way around? It was *totally* real.

'Could I borrow it?' I asked him.

'Borrow it?' he said.

'I don't mean take it away. I just mean have a go in it.'

'All right,' he said, 'if you can get the kids off it.'

They were on it non-stop, apparently, but not playing a racing game. They had this other thing where they just drove around the English countryside. Not racing, just driving. They played it all day, by all accounts.

So anyway, we turfed them off, I got in, and I did at least get to experience Le Mans. I learnt the circuit layout. I figured out the banked corners and overall got a good feel for the track. It was, all in all, a decent way to get a taste of the circuit.

When I'd finished, I got out, and my mate asked me how it had gone.

'Great,' I said.

He was beaming with pride, and with good reason: his was a great simulator. Now it's coming, the confession bit, because he said, 'I bet it's just as good as the ones you were used to at McLaren, isn't it?'

'Oh yeah, mate,' I said, 'Are you kidding? It's right up there.' *Which was a lie.*

Fair's fair, though, it was better than the first simulator I ever used at Benetton, which was static. It was basically a racing car tub, like an F1 car without the suspension. You got in it the same way. The seat was the same. Steering wheel the same. You had a screen in front of you. But nothing moved, so you didn't really get a feel for anything. There were no vibrations, nothing like that. It was just static.

I guess it was good to get used to the circuit, but aside from that, it didn't really help me in any way: there was no feedback so you couldn't work on set-up. Plus the room they put it in smelled of socks.

All in all, it was pretty useless, so I ended up giving that and all other simulators a wide berth wherever possible.

Arriving at McLaren in 2010 my heart sank when they were like, 'Right, you have to drive the simulator.'

Maybe they'd got wind of my severe simulator aversion because they'd even put it in my contract that I had to drive the simulator before and after every race (as far as I know I was a pioneer in that regard, because everybody now has that clause in their contract).

'We'll work you gently into it,' they said, 'because everybody gets sick in the simulator.'

I was still thinking of the bathtub thing with the arcade-game screen. 'Really?' I said, 'what sort of simulator have you got then?'

'Oh, it's pretty good,' they said, 'we've spent about thirty million on it.'

Okay.

So I go into this really dark room. It smells a bit musty, there's no air in there, and there's a carbon-fibre tub of the car you get into which is on widthways rails, so it goes side to side. Full-on massive surround screen. *Toto*, I'm thinking, *I have a feeling we're not in Kansas any more.*

Besides that is a whole bunch of other screens for the various engineers: the simulator engineer, the tyre engineer, the engine engineer, the engineer engineer, who all sit behind the driver.

And they were right: everybody feels sick. Remember when you were a kid and you used to get in your dad's car and want to throw up? It's like that. Motion sickness, it is. The driver's sick. All those poor engineers sitting behind the screens feel sick, too.

Still. Unappetising as it was, it did the job – the job being to successfully mimic all aspects of driving a Formula One car, even the G-force, which comes through a crash helmet you wear. This thing is connected to the machine in order to simulate G-force which it does so well that you think, *If that goes wrong, it's going to rip my head off.*

Also, it has a system in it that makes it vibrate, so every gear-shift you do, you get a jolt in the right manner. If you lock a tyre under-braking, you can feel it lock; with oversteer, you can feel the car slide, which is frankly amazing, because it's very difficult to 'feel' a rear end that isn't actually there. How can you feel wheels and tyres that don't exist? And yet somehow you can.

They also have the real brakes, so even though there's no wheel and thus no brake disc, there's a calliper so it feels identical to the race car. It was so close to the real thing that when you crashed you'd close your eyes and take your hands off the steering wheel.

Even so, at first I was bit sniffy. 'The brakes don't feel right.'

Next time I went in there they had the brakes sorted.

They'd make a change to the suspension and you'd feel it. Later, when you climbed in the real thing, it would be *exactly the same* as the simulator and you'd be left wondering what kind of witchcraft they used to do that.

So it was a great simulator. I think most of them still aren't as good as McLaren's. It had everything.

And yet… it didn't. Some days I'd get in it and be completely jubilant. 'It feels really good; it's identical to what the car feels like,' and I'd be brimming with confidence that we could find a set-up that would work for the next race.

Sure enough, we'd have a great day in the simulator, use the set-up for the next race, Bob's your uncle, Fanny's your aunt, and then the next time I went in there, it would feel utter shite, nothing like reality, and we could never work out why.

The team would be like, 'Well, there's nothing different, mate. It's the same. It's just you getting in it *thinking* it's different.'

I'd go, 'No, it's different.'

Every driver was the same. We'd spend three hours trying to correlate with reality – all to no avail.

Then, of course, you had the fact that circuits were different. Or there would be changes to the tyre compound, and we'd have to correlate the simulator to the new tyres, which again you'd think was weird because it hasn't got any tyres on it, but it does in the simulator.

It was one of the things that if the simulator was working then it was amazing, an invaluable tool. But when it wasn't working? It just sucked time and money, frayed tempers, wore everyone out, stopped being any kind of tool at all and became a hindrance instead.

And it was funny, because I'd turn up at a race, and I'd speak to Nico Rosberg. 'How much simulator have you done?' He'd go, 'Never used one,' and then go out and win the race. Although to be fair he did have the quickest car.

There were certain drivers who despite being contracted to go in the simulator were jammy gits, managed to wheedle out and only went in it about twice a year – naming no names Fernando Alonso.

But frankly you couldn't blame them. Who in their right mind would want to spend unnecessary time in this small, airless room, redolent with the promise of imminent vomit? My thoughts went out to the guy whose sole job it was to look after the simulator. He'd been my data engineer and then became the simulator engineer. I don't know if that's a searing indictment of how bad it was to be my data engineer or not. I dread to think.

Just the regular drivers and test drivers were allowed to use the simulator. Then you had other teams, such as Force India, who would pay to use it. Only then it all went hush-hush, because all our data would have to be kept separate from their data. Their engineers would ask our engineers, 'How does this bit work?' and our engineers would shrug and go, 'Yeah, dunno…'

And now, with 'eSports' all the rage, competition simulator driving has really taken off. They don't use the F1 set-up but they have rigs that are probably just as advanced as my mate has in his living room, and they take part in all sorts of competitions on games like *iRacing, Project Cars 2, Gran Turismo, rFactor 2* and *DiRT 2.0*. They even have teams run by actual Formula One personnel.

Guess who runs a team? Fernando Alonso. I know, right?

4. WINGS

So you've got your front wing and your rear wing. The job of the front wing is to help front downforce, as well as direct the down-force to the rest of the car and to the rear wing, the idea being that the two works as a package.

And my God they've changed over the years. When you look at the year 2000 cars, they're beautiful because they're so simple.

But they're also square; they're boxes. Over the years they become more curvaceous and compact. You've got the engine in the back, all the radiators and everything and the designers are housing it in this little beautiful bubble, trying to make it as compact as possible, so that the airflow is better underneath and round the bodywork to the rear wing.

The front of the car is obviously most important because that's what directs all the airflow round to the rest of the car. If the front doesn't work, the rest of the car doesn't work. If you look at a picture of a wing from 2009, it's so simple. Just three flaps. A very simple front wing, and a bog-standard rear wing to match.

And the reason for that is not because the field of aerodynamics was in the dark ages in 2009 but because it was the first year of a new regulation. See, the thing is that the FIA are constantly introducing new rules, which limits what aerodynamicists are able to do, because otherwise downforce levels get crazy, overtaking becomes even more difficult, and the spectacle of the sport suffers (whole other arguments for another time here that we'll neatly sidestep).

Now, in 2008, the cars were proper extreme. It was like the collective aerodynamicists of Formula One were all under the influence of the same bizarre hallucinogen. We had winglets everywhere. Wings upon wings. We had flicks and scoops and horns.

The following year, then, was like a Year Zero for wings. Regulations curbing their overuse meant that simple was once again in fashion. So what happened? The designers found a way to circumvent, bypass or otherwise sidestep the rules. Not breaking them. Oh no. Just *bending* them. Finding a way to gain an advantage while still obeying them. That, after all, is their job.

And so gradually you got this situation where the mad wings crept back, until the 2017 regulations allowed the teams to get even more imaginative, and the designers started dropping acid again (I'm talking to you, Mercedes T-Wing, which is in fact a pretty cool-looking wing).

Look at a wing in Formula One in 2019 and it's just crazy busy. You look at it and you think, if one of those things break, the rest of the car looks like it would be undriveable, because it's so integral to the car.

Again, the Mercedes wing is incredibly detailed. Just by looking at it, you can see the idea of it is for the airflow to go around the front tyre and then be sucked in behind the front tyre to the rest of the aero part, so it's giving you front downforce, it's helping all the way down the middle of the car, it's helping the rear wing, it's helping the full airflow. What's called a Y250 vortex comes off the side of the front wing and connects everything.

That's about as technical as it gets for me. I am not an aero-dynamics expert, but I love the design of what they come up with. I love the fact that they're not making the car beautiful to make it beautiful, they're making it beautiful because that's how it looks when you design a car aerodynamically. I've got a McLaren P1 road car and it's stunning to look at, but it's not designed to be beautiful, it's just beautiful because that's how it looks when the aerodynamics are working at their best.

5. LET'S HEAR IT FOR THE POOR, OVERLOOKED WIND TUNNEL

When Ross Brawn bought out Honda and Brawn Racing was born in 2009, I found myself rescued from a potentially sticky career situation and sitting in a car, the BGP 001, that looked very, very tasty indeed.

We were a newcomer team, and despite the fact that in Ross we had an engineer who'd already won multiple Championships with Benetton and Ferrari, and despite the fact that every single person in that team had been racing for years, whether as an engineer, aerodynamicist, or a mechanic, nobody really expected us to be competitive.

But that's because they didn't know what we knew, which was that Ross had been working on something that would capitalise on a 2009 regulation change, having spotted a loophole in the rules. He'd put a 'double diffuser' on the car. A diffuser is a bit of underbody aimed at aiding the passage of air from underneath and out the back, converting it from the low, downforce-creating pressure beneath the car to the natural pressure of the outside air, and reducing drag at the back. And this one did that job, only twice as well.

Like I say, our rivals didn't know about that. So when I then went on to win six of the first seven races of the 2009 season, I think it's fair to say that we caught the competition napping and they spent much of the season playing catch-up.

History tells us that Brawn ended up winning the Driver's and the Constructor's Championships that season, of course, so all's well that ends well. But the fact is that given our huge head start, it was a little bit touch and go at the end there. We didn't fully capitalise on the massive gap we'd opened up on the other teams.

Why? Two words: wind tunnel.

Other teams spend something like £14m or £15m in the wind tunnel per year. At Brawn – new and comparatively under-funded – we were spending something like £500,000.

And time in the wind tunnel is so important. We may have started with a great car but development throughout any year is key and we weren't doing that. Other teams did. It's a huge strength at Red Bull, and sure enough they made up an enormous amount of lap time that season because they'd spent so much in the wind tunnel.

McLaren. Again, they were a second and a half slower than us at the first race but made up ground over the season, going on to beat us twice and almost winning the last race but for a brake failure.

Brawn? We changed the front wing once. Other than that, the design we started with was the one we finished with. Lucky it was such a good package.

A simulator doesn't teach you much about the car. It's mostly for the driver to get his eye in and help do set-up changes. Mainly it's just a case of confirming what the data is already telling you. So you're not actually learning anything. Whereas, a wind tunnel is everything, it really is, for the simple reason that aerodynamics is the most important thing in an F1 car. They will help the mechanical grip, the cooling of the engine, determine the visibility for the driver. Everything is determined by aerodynamics, because it's all about downforce. And that comes from the wind tunnel.

6. THE VEXED QUESTION OF SET-UP

Not really a bit of 'kit' as such, but so closely related that it might as well go here anyway. In terms of set-up, we'd do some of it in the simulator. Also, we'd carry it over from the previous race, or the team understands which circuits are similar and which are completely different.

Again, they run simulations – and I'm not talking about the simulator that we drive, but computer-based simulations – of what it should feel like with certain set-ups. It's all very useful and we'd arrive at the circuit with a pretty good set-up most of the time. Put it this way, it would be very unusual for us to turn up and think, *Hang on, we're totally out of bed here and we need to change significant things.*

Sometimes you'd have to change big things. Like maybe the suspension geometry – the various aspects that make up the suspension, like camber, toe and 'caster angle' – wasn't working, which would take up to two hours. You make the changes and you think it's okay. Oh, but it's still a bit pants and you have to go back to the drawing board. Or the aerodynamics just aren't working – we're not getting the downforce that we expected. Why is that? And then they have to run through all the checks and sensors to find out what's wrong.

A lot of this will be going on behind the scenes while we drivers are still munching on healthy snacks in our motorhomes. Then we get in the car, tell them how it feels, and the next phase starts: how can we make this car better for the race weekend?

I'll take the car out. *Oh, there's too much understeer at high speed, traction's terrible*, so we'd add a front wing, change the ride height, whatever was needed.

It was mad, the amount of time we spend with the engineers developing the car over the weekend. But then for some races, it's like, *Hang on, this feels great*, and you adjust the front wing one or two degrees and that's it for the weekend. Sometimes cars work on certain circuits and not on others and that was the fun thing in the 2018 F1 season: some races Mercedes were amazing, and other races Ferrari were amazing and then you had Red Bull that were quick in other places. But this year, 2019, it's all Mercedes. They're quick everywhere, which is demoralising for everyone else because they don't have a weakness. Or, if they do, they're not showing it.

Sometimes you'll get to the point where it feels great, but you wonder if it feels too great. Do we need to reduce downforce? If we did that we'll be quicker on the straights but the trade-off is that we'll be slower on the corners. And is that a trade-off we're willing to make?

This happened at Spa, for example, in 2012, when I qualified on pole, and went on to win. The car already felt perfect but we still thought there were improvements we could make. Sometimes that can be a bad thing, of course – if it ain't broke, don't fix it – but on that occasion it worked.

Spa's probably my favourite circuit – just shading it over Suzuka – and it's because it's so smooth and flowing. By tweaking the car to fit the circuit and complement my style we got a perfect synthesis of the two. I'm grinning now, just thinking about it.

Funny. We never had any involvement with design. The only thing that I would work on was the cockpit. Is it okay to have this switch here? Can we put the fire extinguisher here? Where do you want your CD changer?

And for me, because I was the tallest driver: are the pedals okay here? Would you like them further away? Narrower? Further apart?

Aside from that? Nada. You got what you were given. As a driver your input was solely in the cockpit, the simulator and then after practice and testing. It doesn't have enough rear downforce. It's oversteery in high-speed corners. I want grip here, I want grip there. My rear's feeling delicate, matron.

You'll spend time in the wind tunnel talking about aerodynamics and they'll design you a new front wing. *Wahey, I've got a new front wing*, you think.

'It's going to give us this amount of downforce at the front. You'll have much more front grip as you turn into the corner.'

'Awesome. So what will happen with the rear grip at the exit?'

'You'll lose grip at the exit, yes.'

Not so awesome.

You really need to keep your wits about you when you're driving in order to take note of what's wrong and what's right about the car; equally you need to become adept at articulating that to the team. You'll feed back to the engineers and in return you hear, 'Well, okay, it's in the pipeline, it's coming in a few weeks,' but that might not be soon enough for you, so you end up trading something else you want done in the hope that you'll get your oversteer sorted a race earlier.

In short, there are a million things going on at once, developments being made all the time.

It's a constant quest for perfection. For the rest of us, it's about always trying to learn, and if you think you're weaker than your teammate somewhere, you're right into the guts of that. 'Guys, show me why he's so quick through that corner. Is it the set-up?'

'No, it's the same car you're driving.'

'Okay, well what's he doing differently? I need to see this.'

So you look at the data – the throttle traces, the braking traces, the steering traces, gears, there's everything you need to learn from your teammate, and suddenly you're not so much a racing driver as a detective in a constant quest to be your best.

7. TYRES

Question: what do racing divers think and talk about more than anything else? Yes, it's tyres. And that goes for any class of racing, but especially Formula One. Are we talking about how much we love the tyres? How great they are? No, we're not. We're *complaining* about the tyres.

In F1 it used to be the case that we had Bridgestone and Michelin who were in competition with each other, meaning that some teams were on Bridgestone and some teams were on Michelin, which meant that the two manufacturers worked night and day to make better tyres, each of them trying to outdo the other, and because of this healthy competition they came up with softer, better, more consistent tyres. It was awesome.

Old timers like me can remember all the way back to 2004, which was a great year for tyre wars, so the cars were super quick and there was very little degradation of the tyres. They were great tyres because the manufacturers were fighting each other.

Nowadays – not so good. Since 2011 Pirelli has been the sole supplier of tyres for F1 – and because there's no competition, there has, in my opinion, not been such an emphasis on development, and the tyres have *arguably* not been as good. Whatever the reason, I think that every driver in F1 has a whinge about the Pirelli tyres.

The problem is that nobody really understands them. We don't get why sometimes you can get it in the temperature working range and it feels good while at other times it just doesn't work. One race, the temperature for the tyres should be *x*, and in that range it's really good. You go to the next race and in that range, they just don't work.

As a result the tyres we have now are probably two to two-and-a-half seconds slower than we had back in the golden age of 2004.

In Super GT, we have four tyre manufacturers: Yokohama, Dunlop, Michelin and Bridgestone, which is great. They're all trying to outdo each other so you go testing and it's just non-stop tyres all weekend long. You've got brand-new tyres literally being flung at you the whole time (not *literally*, that would hurt, but you know what I mean) and it's great; you're testing 12 different types of Bridgestone all of differing construction. This one's a bit softer. This one's a bit stiffer. This one has a different tread pattern. This one plays a happy tune.

I love all that. Given that much choice you can really tailor your tyres to your specific needs, while the chances are you'll be on completely different tyres from your competitor. Plus it's just great fun trying out all these new sets of tyres – until you get to the end of testing and they want your feedback, that is. I'm like, 'Are you kidding me? It's like twelve sets of tyres, how am I supposed to remember all of them?'

But even if we're not complaining about tyres, then we're talking about them: what tyres to use, how warm they are. The tyres we call slicks are the tyres that are made for dry-weather conditions. They have no groove (which is why we're not allowed them on road cars) and in wet weather you won't get any grip. The water can't go anywhere. It just touches the flat surface and you just slide, whereas with a grooved tyre the wet goes through the tyre and you get grip on the roads.

There are lots of variables, of course. The warmth, which you achieve initially with a tyre warmer and then by getting out on the track; the pressure, although there'll be a minimum pressure you can run on the tyres, which Pirelli will give you because they don't want you running it too low and risk damaging the tyre or getting a puncture.

Also, you have to run two different tyre compounds in the race. Every race weekend you have to run, let's say, a soft tyre and a medium tyre or, if they've brought a medium and a super soft, you have to run one of each in a race. You can't run just one set of tyres for the whole race, you have to run both, which means that some people might start the race on a soft, some people might start on a medium and then they get to the pit stop and have to swap over. It makes the race more interesting.

What I really like, too, is how the teams know how much tread is left on the tyre. They have some kind of gadget that actually tells them. It's amazing. Plus of course you can see for yourself. The thing to look out for is 'graining', which is when the tyre is worn or damaged and you get a ripple effect, which in turn means a lot less tyre touching the circuit – because it's rippled, you get a lot less grip. That happens mainly on the slicks.

If you get graining on the front, it cleans up. On the rears, it doesn't often clean up, so if you start getting graining on the rear, you're in trouble and you would have to pit.

A lot of it is about looking after the tyres. You might be on a strategy that involves pitting later, so you don't just go flat out from the word go, because you'll damage the tyres by lap five, so instead you're looking after them by braking for a corner a little bit more gently, not putting too much heat into the rear tyre. You'll exit the corner and the first throttle application will either be a little bit later or a little bit more gentle to stop wheel spin on the rear tyres. Or if it's a front tyre issue, you enter high-speed corners being that bit more gentle with the steering or go in a little bit slower.

That's what I loved about F1. It was always more than just being the quickest from A to B. So if my stint was 25 laps long I'd let the guy in front pull away, knowing that he was going to destroy his tyres. He might pull away and three or four seconds later the team would be, like, 'Are you okay? Is everything okay?' and I'd say, 'Yeah, just looking after the tyres,' and then towards the end of a stint I would start catching and catching and catching and maybe even overtake him before he stops for new tyres.

Another thing: marbles. This is what you get outside of the racing line. When the tyre degrades and it slides, you get bits of the used rubber flick off. We call that marbles, and they flick off all over the circuit, meaning that off the racing line there are marbles all over the track.

This means that if you have to make an overtaking move, it can be difficult, because you get on the marbles and they're more slippery than the normal circuit. You've dived down the inside, you think, *Oh, I should brake here,* but the problem is the marbles, so you've got less grip than you think. Also, if you brake late for a corner, you run wide, you go on the marbles, you come back on, it takes two or three corners before you can clean your tyres and you get the proper grip back.

It also used to be the case that you could run lots of camber, which is the angle of the tyre affecting the surface area of the tyre that meets the circuit. If the tyre's standing up straight, i.e., not much camber, you'll have a lot of the tyre on the circuit on the straight but then the track turns and the tyre is at an angle and you lose grip. If you're running lots of camber it means you get to the corner and you turn in and you get more front grip. By the same token, if the rear tyres have more camber, it's more stable at the rear, so you go through a long corner, you get on the throttle and, if you have camber, the rear grip stays good, whereas if the tyres were stood up straight with no camber, you won't have as much rear grip, so you'll have oversteer.

That being the case, in F1 you try and run as much camber as you can, and with Michelin and Bridgestone you could play around with it a lot more; you could run different pressures and temperatures, you could mess around with everything.

Pirelli? Not so much. They're, like, *No, you can't do any of that,* because they've had tyre failures and they don't want tyre failures. I guess it looks bad for the brand.

So they've limited everything. You can only go so far with the rear tyre camber, front tyre camber; you have to run a certain pressure, you have to run a certain temperature. This was another area we could really play with in F1, and suddenly it's gone.

But wait, I'm about to get all fair's fair and even-handed on your ass, because while there is indeed a lot of frustration aimed at Pirelli, you've got to say also that Pirelli is the only tyre manufacturer that's willing to be there, and despite taking a lot of flak are still there, plugging away. And, after all, I do think they've improved. And the fact is, that we're always going to whinge about the tyres, because they're the most important thing in a way, they're the things that are touching the ground, the *only* things that touch the ground.

Three Races Where Tyres Really Mattered

Hungary, 2006
Driving for Honda, I'd qualified fourth but we had an engine failure in practice and then I got a ten-place penalty, so I started 14th.

Yeah. I know.

So anyway, it was wet and it was all about fighting through. It was me, Michael Schumacher and Fernando Alonso all fighting the whole time because they'd been penalised, too, so like a bunch of naughty schoolboys we all started near the back and fought our way through, meaning that it was a hell of a battle to the front.

As the circuit dried out, it was about looking after the tyres, but still making the moves when catching the leaders. Then came the all-important tyre change, because once again we moved to slicks at the right time and that was it, I was in the lead and I was radioing in, saying, 'What's the gap for the guy behind me?'

'Thirty-five seconds,' they said.

I was, like, 'Wow, okay, that's quite a big gap,' and then I just enjoyed the last ten laps of the race. I didn't want it to end, it went by way too fast.

The last few laps, I'd backed it off and just cruised in and I was radioing into the team, 'Is everything okay with the car? Do I need to do anything?' They said, 'No, it's all okay,' and I clinched my first victory.

Silverstone, 2009
This, you will remember, was the Championship year, me racing for Brawn, Silverstone the eighth round, and I was out in front, leading my teammate Rubens Barrichello by 26 points, with Red Bull Sebastian in third.

I arrived full of anticipation, thinking this could be *my* year, but we got there and it was cold and it stayed cold all the way through testing. My times were poor, Rubens was beating me, and I couldn't understand why. How come I was being so slow and he was being so quick? Until the team pointed out that my tyre temperatures were way lower than his. Why couldn't I get the heat into my tyres and he could? Because of the difference in our driving styles: mine, smooth and precise; his, aggressive. I ended up qualifying sixth (and only by the skin of my teeth). The race then became a case of me trying to work out how to drive on my tyres, which I did, but all too late and nowhere near the podium finish I'd been hoping for.

Monaco, 2009

I got away in the lead and pulled a good gap. It was clear that Rubens, in second, would be damaging his rear tyres by following closely, so I just took it easy on the tyres on entry, accelerating gently, limiting wheel spin so that my tyres were in much better condition than his, because he was following so closely.

By the middle of the race, I'd pulled a good gap and then I backed it off for the last stint and just drove it home. But the funny thing is, however easy you go in Monaco, it's still proper scary, because of the walls and in Monaco, especially when you're leading, the circuit just seems to get narrower and narrower and narrower as you get more and more tired. I mean, you physically get tired, but mentally it's so draining, the focus you need.

CHAMPAGNE SPRAYING IS ALL IN THE THUMB

1. THE WINNING

So, not only have you managed to get signed, bought a boat, a motorhome and have amassed a garage full of cars that cost you a fortune on tax, insurance and storage, but you've only gone and won a bloody race. Here's everything I know about what to do next.

It's never a good look to start the celebrations before you've actually won

It's Canada, 1991, Nigel Mansell is on the home run, cruising to victory, when he starts waving to the crowd.

'Nigel, don't wave to the crowd too soon there, buddy,' remarks a commentator, and they're prophetic words, because Nigel's revs drop, his engine cuts out and that's it, his race is over.

It's been said that Nigel – 'our Nige' – knocked the ignition switch while waving to fans, which would be gutting for him if it were true, although as to whether it is, I couldn't say. Point being, don't go too early. Don't celebrate until you know you've got it. Rule One.

A similar thing happened at the Brazilian Grand Prix in 2008 (yet another race that was very dependent on tyres, in this case, the swapping from wet to dry and then back again). In order to win that year's Championship, Felipe Massa, in a Ferrari, needed to win the race with McLaren's Lewis lower than fifth.

As a result, the race was a proper nail-biter (although my car caught fire, so I had other things on my mind), not least for Lewis who didn't fare well in the pit stops.

Cut to the chase, though, and Massa crossed the line in first with Lewis back in sixth, which, as it stood, meant that Massa had clinched the Championship, not Lewis.

Sure enough, the cameras went to the Ferrari garage, which erupted into the kind of rapturous celebration that shakes the camera because it's being jostled. Except that this was one of those premature celebrations I'm talking about, because back out on the track Lewis was busy snatching back a Championship-winning place. Indeed, on the very last corner of the last lap of the last race, he took fifth, making him the Champion, and not Massa.

In the McLaren garage they went nuts. Back in the Ferrari garage their own celebration died on the vine, just like that. The blood drained from their crestfallen faces. Their heads went into their hands. One of the Ferrari guys was so pissed off that he headbutted a marketing stand, and it is said that Ferrari president Luca di Montezemolo was so cheesed off that he destroyed the television he was watching (although Ferrari still won the Constructor's, so come on, mate, keep things in perspective, eh?).

You get out of the car very quickly when you've won

Your steering wheel comes off, safety straps unbuckle, headrest unplugs, you jump out and you're on the car and you're just, like, 'Hell, yeah!'

At the same time, you're looking around and you see your team, and they're going wild and you're giving them the full beam while at the same time you're looking for specific people, whether it's friends, family, whatever, and you wave at them and you wave at the crowd, who are hopefully cheering for you and not booing you (we'll talk about Monza in a bit) although it doesn't really matter because you've still got your helmet on and nothing could penetrate that bubble of joy anyway. And then you run over to the team, jump on them and they're all kissing your helmet – your crash helmet – and then you get dragged away to do the rest of your stuff.

And that's what it's like to win.

Have a signature celebration

I did the winner. Arms up, number one finger. I'd do that to my dad and he'd do it back to me in reply. I'd be out of the car in five seconds (see above, and see also, *we don't talk about crashes*) arms up, finger aloft. Even in the excitement of the moment, with my helmet on and well-wishers jostling me, I could always pick my dad out in the crowd. It was that father–son bond.

That and the fact he always wore a pink shirt.

Mind how you go in the podium room

In the last six years or so they've had cameras in the pre-podium room. There you are, about to bowl into the podium room for a breather before the trophy ceremony, and the steward reminds you, 'Don't forget the camera's there, don't swear.'

Other good things to remember about being in the pre-podium room when you're being observed by the entire TV-watching world: don't go flinging your cap around like a spoilt child. If you have an issue with another driver, don't air it there and then. You know, the basics.

Before the days of cameras in the podium room? Now, that's a different story.

At Suzuka in 2011, I'd started in second behind Sebastian in a Red Bull but got up the inside of him on the straight down to turn one. I was about to put him in my mirrors when, *bosh*, he pushed me into the grass, allowing my McLaren teammate Lewis to overtake me on the outside which, if you've been paying attention, you'll know is right up there in the ultimate indignity stakes, along with taking out your teammate and crashing under the safety car.

I thought Sebastian should have been penalised for that. He used the SMIDSY defence: *Sorry, mate, I didn't see you.* So I went up to him in the podium room afterwards.

'Right,' I said, 'so that's how it's going to be is it? We're going to be pushing and shoving each other off the circuit.'

'Hmm,' he said with furrowed brow, 'What do you mean?'

I said, 'Turn one, you pushed me on to the grass.'

He said, 'There was no penalty. This means I did nothing wrong.'

I said, 'Mate, you know you did something wrong.'

He still looked confused.

'Okay,' I said. 'Fine. If we're going to be like that, fair enough, let it be.'

Now, as confrontations go, it was hardly Bromley Wetherspoons on a Saturday night, but that was about as angry as it got. And it was all forgotten about in the next nanosecond because even though I'd won the race he'd won the Championship and we both had the all-important business of celebrations to attend to.

Thinking about it, there were quite a lot of times in 2011 when I spoke to Sebastian. I might had had a word with him after the incident at Spa in 2010, when I was defending my Championship and holding second in the race, and he lost control and virtually T-boned me, putting us both out of contention and thus putting a massive dent in my chances of the Championship.

He was one, like Max, who calmed down as a driver. I think he probably just realised that he was messing up too much. He was in that period of his career where he was super quick, but was in the habit of pushing it too far and making mistakes.

In Max's case, he had the team saying to him, 'Max, you can't do that, you can't just throw the car up the inside and cause accidents', and whereas before he was just shrugging his shoulders and refusing to change his driving style, he's taken those comments on board, is finishing every race and doing a bloody great job.

The art of champagne spraying is all in the thumb

The champagne we have for Middle Eastern races is actually rose water. It doesn't fizz properly and it tastes horrible, but you still have to play the game – you have to swig it, even if it tastes horrid.

Watch Kimi Räikkönen, who likes a drink, when he's on a podium in a Middle Eastern race. You can see his face, it's like, *Ugh*.

Personally, I love a swig on the podium, even if it is only just rose water. I think it's an important part of the show. And if it is champagne then you're so dehydrated after a race that two swigs of it and you're anyone's. You're suddenly a very cheap date.

They take the cork out for you in Formula One, which is luxury, a blue-chip valet service compared to Super GT where you're expected to remove the cork yourself. Now, as a veteran of Monaco Super Mondays, I'm a dab hand at removing corks so it's not a problem for me, but there's a driver called Nick Cassidy who struggles to such an extent that even the presenters have started taking the piss out of him.

I feel for him, actually. You want to be able to go out and enjoy yourself on the podium without having to deal with the extra stress of extracting a cork from a bottle. What's more, it's fizzy sake most of the time. Last year our team appeared on the podium four times, and it was sake each time. It's sticky, sweet and seriously strong but I stick to my ritual of always taking a swig.

My teammate Naoki Yamamoto doesn't touch alcohol but won the Super Formula Championship last year, and every single driver on the podium covered him with champagne, poor guy. Or was it sake? Either way, he wasn't happy.

In Formula One, all you have to do is stick your thumb over the end, and it's so big – a jeroboam, which is four bottles in one – that spraying is awesome just as long as you make sure to a.) get your thumb right over the end when you shake and then b.) release a tiny bit to spray, being careful to angle it.

Obvious, you'd think, but in the heat of the moment it's easy to get it wrong and I've seen some drivers shake it up without their thumb over the end, going, 'Wahey!' as it hiccups out of the bottle in a foamy waterfall, completely oblivious to the fact that they've just ruined the spectacle.

So, no, you have to remember your thumb placement, you have to keep on shaking it as you spray and you have to make sure that you soak as many people in the vicinity as you can.

That's very important, that last bit, and you'll need to be quick, catch them unaware, because what you'll find is that while there are a lot of people on the podium at the beginning of the ceremony, they all disappear as soon as you pick up a bottle. In any case, you aim it at the other drivers on the podium. They also have another senior staff member from the team on stage – your engineer or the chief mechanic or something, it's different every race – and so you'll probably try and get them as well, and you'll always try and *really* soak those guys, because you know they've got to go back to work and finish the debrief.

I'm really good at that, even if I do say so myself. The trick is to grab it, turn, and shoot. *Kapow*. Don't give them a moment to think. I'm not saying that I'm competitive about it (of course I'm competitive about it) but I think I'm pretty good at getting people without being got in return, not that it's in any way an extension of the competition on the track (which of course it is).

Plus you spray the guys below, of course. Guess who I'd always be aiming for? That's right, my dad again! He was my bullseye. Even now I can picture his face down below, laughing.

You have your interviews, too, of course. We'd have an ex-Formula One driver or a celebrity come up and do it. It was fun if it was a celebrity, but only if they knew a little about the sport, which was relatively rare; better was when it was an ex-driver, someone like DC who you could have a good crack with.

Incidentally, it has to be said that in F1 our nickname game is pretty weak, with Christian names – Lewis, Kimi, Sebastian – being the most common informality, and initials like JB and DC reserved for the truly adventurous. That said, Team Button was responsible for one or two good ones, and having been the victim of them at school ('Zipper', 'Jennifer'), I was more than willing to dish them out. Dad became 'Papa Smurf', named after he grew a Papa Smurf-like beard, but perhaps the best one was 'Britney' for Nico Rosberg, because he used to have long, wavy hair. I remember him walking into a night club in Tokyo, spotting our lot and looking very happy to see us until I stood up and yelled, 'Britney! Hit me baby one more time,' across the club at him. The smile turned upside down pretty quickly.

And of course now the world has turned and instead of being the one interviewed, I'm the one likely to do the interview for Sky. I did it at Silverstone, which was the first time I'd ever been on the podium at Silverstone – and if you think I failed to make that joke then you really don't know me at all – talking to winner Lewis, as well as Sebastian and iceman Kimi.

The good thing in a situation like that is that you forget that the whole world is watching, you just think of the people in the vicinity, and it's a special atmosphere for all concerned.

Post-ceremony you have the choice of either dropping your jeroboam over the side for the crew, which is a bit dangerous because it's a long way down – unsure whether health and safety approve, not that I've ever checked – or carting it around with you as you go on to your next round of tasks. You give your cap and your trophy to a team member and will be handed another cap to wear (how many different caps does a driver wear during a Grand Prix weekend? About 50 million) for your post-race press conference, which you'll do while soaked in champagne.

There are lots of questions, obviously, but because emotions are so high it's also a time that you should be at your most guarded, because the last thing you want as a driver is to let your feelings get the better of you and start going off-script and running off at the mouth. Keeping a lid on it at a time like that is far more exhausting than you might imagine.

The whole thing, in fact, is incredibly tiring, and the likelihood is that you'll be absolutely knackered by the time you reach the rest of your team. You're probably more shagged out from the interviews than you are from actually driving the car.

But if you've got any thoughts about coming down then the team will put you right about that, because those guys will be sky high with emotion and adrenalin, and it's a very special occasion when you return to the fold. For your teammates, your arrival is the amazing encore and together you surf that celebratory wave. Which means draining the last of that bottle together.

As for the empty. If you've won the race the chances are you'll want to keep that bottle, and it'll end up in storage somewhere, something to show your disinterested grandchildren. But if you haven't won the chances are that you'll give it away to the team. Same with your podium cap. Honestly, if I'd kept all the caps I'd been given I couldn't keep up with the storage.

Make sure you get to keep your trophy

A lot of drivers have a contract which says the team keeps all the trophies. I know that because I had it at BAR and McLaren and, initially, at Honda as well, although things changed at Honda when it transpired that my teammate, Takuma Sato, didn't like the number four, believing it to be an unlucky number. Having finished third in the previous year's Championship, I was number three, and so he asked me to swap.

I was, like, 'Uh uh, I'm not just going to swap numbers, I finished third in the Championship, so I want the number three that I earned; you didn't even earn the number four – you were eighth – you only got number four because I was number three.'

Or words to that effect. I'm sure I put it more diplomatically than that. Or should I say that I'm sure somebody put it more diplomatically than that on my behalf.

The team said, 'Oh, go on, Jenson, just to keep the peace.'

'No way,' I said.

They said, 'Okay, what can we do to sweeten the deal?'

I said, 'Give me all my trophies. Whatever trophies I win this year, I get to keep.'

And they said, 'Okay. You're on.'

'Great,' I said thinking what a result, because I didn't give a damn about the number four; it was only a number; I just wanted something out of the deal.

So I got my trophies, which cost about £15,000–£25,000 each. Cool. What's more it's not like they deliver them to you in a bit of bubble wrap and brown packing tape. They come packaged in the most gorgeous box. All the trophies are different designs, but the one thing they all have in common is their beautiful presentation boxes.

So a lot of the time – maybe even most of the time – the team will keep the trophies, and if that's the case you do have the option to get a replica made at a cost of £15,000. Having been on the podium 50 times, I drew the line at spending that kind of cash on third- or even second-place trophies, but I do have all of my first-place ones. They're pretty special.

The World Championship trophy is different again, because the trophy changes hands, so you get the same trophy that everybody's had, inscribed with the actual signatures of drivers such as Juan Manuel Fangio, Jack Brabham, Graham Hill, Jackie Stewart, James Hunt, Niki Lauda, Alain Prost, Ayrton Senna. It makes you feel giddy just to look at it.

You have to give it back, though, of course – mine went to Sebastian who won it in 2010, and when I enquired about getting a replica made I was a bit put off by the £35,000 cost, thinking, *Really? Am I really going to pay that much for a trophy?* Until my manager, Richard, bought me one as a gift. Now *that* is a manager.

The Championship year was of course a big one for souvenirs. I've also kept all of my helmets and suits from that year, and of the three cars that were made, I was given one. As I said way back, I took a pay cut to drive for Brawn, as a result of which there were various sweeteners built into the contract, a car being one of them. Mind you, they tried to wheedle out of it, and though the one I've ended up with is one of the proper three with a functional engine, they tried to palm me off with a replica version. 'We'll make you a fourth chassis,' they said. Thing was, they didn't want me showing other people the engine.

'But I'm not going to take a fourth chassis,' I insisted toughly (through a third party). 'I want one of the three that we used.'

'Oh, no, it's not worded like that in the contract.'

'I don't care how it's worded, you know what the deal was.'

In the end they gave in and I got my original car. Ross Brawn has another one, and the third went to Mercedes, the engine supplier

Not that I can start it up, mind you. You don't just turn the ignition key on a Formula One car. No, it would cost me £50,000 to start it up, because I'd need the assistance of three or four people, all the computers and the electronics. It's not the kind of thing you use for popping to the shops.

Ideally I'd like to put it on show here in LA. There's the Petersen Automotive Museum, which is the most beautiful car museum I've ever been to. Seriously, put this book down, Google it, you will not be disappointed. So it would be great if it could go in there. I'll ship it over, they'll look after it, free storage, people get to see it and I get to visit. Something else to show my disinterested grandchildren.

Remember that you still have a job to do

After a race, you go and see the engineers for a debrief while events are still fresh in your mind, and this is something you do whether you came first or last. If it's the latter then you'll be more than happy to escape the scorn and pity of the outside world and shelter among familiar faces in order to lick your wounds.

If it's the former, however, you might well stagger in, plastered already from your three swigs of champagne, at which point you'll share it out into little plastic beakers from the water machine and everything's great fun and very convivial.

The crucial 'but' is that while you're all in a celebratory mood, you still have to remember the debrief bit, because no matter how well the race went, there are still things to improve. You never just say, 'Well, that was a great race, let's do exactly the same thing next time,' because firstly, there's no such thing as a flawless Grand Prix weekend, even if you win, and secondly because the influencing factors are changing all the time. Maybe the pit stop wasn't as quick as it should have been or, 'Are you sure we should have been that late pitting on that set of tyres?' So we'll talk through those issues first, and then go through the whole procedure of the race, from the start to the last lap of the race.

How was the start? Was the clutch working okay? Was the throttle working okay? How was turn one? How were the brakes? Oversteer? Understeer? Any issues within the car that you would like to change? It's a whole menu of things that you run through which takes at least an hour and a half, and only then do you…

Party afterwards

Winning the Monaco Grand Prix is fun, because you go to a special after-party, a black tie do attended by the royal family. I ended up dragging everybody to a club afterwards, thinking,

'Hang on a minute, I'm a bloke from Somerset, and I've just won the Monaco Grand Prix and now I'm in the Amber Lounge partying with Prince Albert.'

And the whole time I was half-expecting my mum to shake me awake, going, 'Jenson, Jenson, you're late for school...'

2. THE LOSING

Losing's a funny thing in F1. Even though the perception of the sport is that of the driver as winner or loser, it's really much more of a team thing, so you do at least share that burden – maybe even more so than you share the glory of winning, if I'm guiltily honest about it.

How do you define *losing*? That's the first thing to consider. After all, you turn up to a race weekend knowing that one of the top three will win. You have to go back to the opening race of the 2013 season to find a race where the winning constructor was anyone other than Mercedes, Ferrari, or Red Bull. It was Kimi for Lotus, and that itself was a complete anomaly, the first time it had happened since 2009, when I won the Championship, when it was us, Red Bull, McLaren and Ferrari in contention. That's very nearly a decade of total stranglehold at the top.

With that in mind, those outside the top three are forced to revisit their expectations of what it means to win and also, it follows, to lose. So losing, then, is no longer 'not winning', it has become 'doing worse than expected'.

So if you approach the weekend knowing you're capable of fifth, and you finish ninth or tenth, or you don't score any points at all, that's horrific. That's losing. It's all about your expectations of yourself, the car, the team – about what you know you can achieve in the circumstances versus what you actually do achieve.

What really hurt was when you were expected to fight for a position and you were a long way off. Or if the car just didn't perform. An accident? Well, shit happens, as Forrest Gump said. But when you've actually got a serious issue with the car and it's just not working, that's like shit that *shouldn't* happen. It's the point at which you start having meetings that go on forever, sucking up time and brainspace, hoovering up all the heart and passion you had for the battle. You never see teams more collectively despondent than when technical gremlins have ruined the weekend.

As for how you feel as the driver when you don't do as well as you'd hoped? How do I feel? Well, the answer is pretty down and frustrated. I don't normally raise my voice, but it has happened and it's happened in situations like that, because what really grinds my gears is hearing that we're quick, that our car is great and that we should be winning. You go through four or five races, and each time they say the same thing. 'Yeah, we're this quick, we're this good, we've got the best car.' And yet you keep finishing eighth.

It was at times like that that I may have let my frustrations get the better of me. 'Solve these problems, and stop saying we're good when we're not. We clearly do have issues, and instead of sticking our heads in the sand we need to work out what they are and how we can solve them, because right now it's embarrassing.'

Jenson's pissed off. Jenson hardly ever gets pissed off.

'We're tweaking. We're tweaking.'

'No, we need to make a big change. We need to make a big change in order to find our performance.'

Then we get to Monaco, and, 'This is the one for us, we're going to be quick here, because we don't have the power, but it doesn't matter so much around Monaco.'

Except that you go and finish worse than you did the last race.

'Come on, guys, we've just proved that we don't have the best car.'

By which time they might decide to listen, and you're already several races behind.

In many ways I think it's realising where you are that's the most important thing in F1. We're the fifth-best team but we have issues and we've got to work on it. And that means accepting that you're the fifth-best team, not thinking you're the third best. You've got to realise where you stand and what you need to do to improve.

I remember being at BAR, Honda or Brawn and knowing what the other teams were up to. Little details we could find out about them, what they were bringing to the next race, what improvements they'd made to the car, major set-up changes, things like that.

Then I moved to McLaren. I was, like, 'So, do we know what other people are doing? Do we understand how their car's going to look?'

They looked at one another. 'No. How are we going to know that?'

'Well, every other team I've been at has had an interest in other teams. They make sure they know what other teams are up to.'

They said, 'No, we've never done that.'

I think it was because they thought they were the best, so why would they need to understand what other people were doing? But in the smaller teams, there was always a way of finding out what other teams are doing and learning from it, which was always quite fun.

After all, the competition never stops, because there's always something to play for. All the teams get money for taking part in the Championship. It's not quite as clear-cut as saying that the better they do the more money they get, because Ferrari always gets the most thanks to a special 'Ferrari' payment, but it more or less runs along those lines: the top ten get an 'equal share' payment of around $42m, and then there are performance payouts, a 'Constructor's Championship bonus fund', 'historic payments' and the aforementioned 'Ferrari payment' to take into consideration.

It's all very complicated, which I'm sure suits a lot of people fine, but what it does mean is that a top four Championship place is worth a lot of money (Ferrari will get well over $200m), while a number ten place should be worth at least $50m.

Anything below that, though, and you might want to think about taking on a paper round to help with the rent.

It is, of course, a vicious and ever-decreasing circle, because the less money you're given, the fewer resources you have to develop the car for the next year. One bad year and a team can find themselves spiralling out of control.

All of which is a roundabout way of saying that even if you're having a terrible season and it feels like the best thing to do is concentrate your aim on the following season, you can't. You have to keep on pushing.

Okay, maybe – now I come to think about it – if there was a massive rule change coming, then perhaps the team might think, 'Hang on, there's no point in working on this, we should develop the new car more, spend more time on that.' But aside from that scenario you'd work tirelessly all the way through the season to develop your car because, firstly, you can't afford not to and, secondly, because you can carry most of that development work into the next season. The tub might be different, but a lot of the stuff you will test and if it works, you'll put it on the next year's car as well.

I think that I found it easier to deal with loss, defeat and failure when I was younger. These days, if I have a bad race it hurts on some kind of weird primal level because I start thinking, 'Okay, am I as good as I used to be? Am I over the hill?'

This happens in Super GT now, of course. Not long ago I had a bad weekend, running in fifth, my pace not quite what

I wanted it to be, and then ended up in a crash with someone and came away with no points.

But it wasn't the crash that annoyed me; it was the fact that I was off the pace. I left thinking, *What am I doing?*

And *Am I as good as I used to be?*

And *Is all this worth it, for how I feel right now?*

You end up asking yourself not just if you're not the driver you used to be, but how much less good you're prepared to be before you jack it all in. I find myself wondering how mentally tough am I to accept that dip in quality? Can I accept that dip in quality? Can I accept *any* dip in quality?

After all, I'm a driver who asks a lot of myself. My biggest and toughest rival is the guy in the mirror.

It's one of the reasons fitness is so important to me. A lot of sportsmen as they age will let their fitness go, and that to me goes hand in hand with throwing in the towel, which I'm not prepared to do yet.

On the other hand, do I want to be that guy who carries on well past his sell-by date, churning out less and less impressive results?

Sometimes you see amazing comebacks. David Beckham appeared in a Manchester United Treble Reunion match and scored a brilliant goal with the last kick of the game. But for every one of those there's a dozen failed or fizzled-out comeback stories, and while there are always highs, it's the lows that hit you hardest.

I feel that now, in Super GT. In 2018 we won a race and carved out a Championship win, which was amazing. But it's the lows – like that zero-pointer – that really hurt me.

3. HATS AND HELMETS:
THE FACTS

Fact: a helmet is not a hat

Actual conversation: 'You know that hat you wear, with all the colours on it?'

'My cap?'

'No, it's not a cap. It doesn't have a peak. The other one.'

'Um…'

'Oh, you know the one. It's got all the colours on it.'

'Oh, wait. Is it quite a bulbous thing, made of like a hard shell?'

'Yes!'

'And it has a visor that comes down over my eyes like this?'

'Yes!'

'That's a helmet.'

'Yes, that's it. Your helmet hat.'

Fact: snapbacks are taking the piss

Monaco, 2017. I was making the grand comeback, as detailed earlier. The team presented me with two caps to wear. One of them was a baseball cap, the sort I'd been wearing my entire career. The other was like a baseball cap, but a sort of flat-peaked and starchy version. The kind you see in gift shops at theme parks – like a baseball cap before it's been properly worn in.

I looked at it, the way you might regard a dead rat on your dinner plate. 'What's that?'

'That's a snapback,' I was told, like I was in the presence of something new and great. And now it made sense: the caps that I'd seen Lewis and Daniel Ricciardo wearing. They weren't just nobby-looking box-fresh baseball caps, they were actually *supposed to look like that*. Jesus.

'No, mate, I'll have the cap,' I said.

Apologies if you're a snapback cap fan – each to their own, and I'm not immune to terrible fashion choices myself – but to me they just look bloody stupid. They don't even look like they fit properly. They blow off too easily because the huge peaks act like sails. Some people even put their ears inside them, for the full 'I bought this in the Harry Potter Experience' effect.

No, for me it's the baseball cap, arched peak. In fact, I employ someone whose sole job is to arch my baseball cap peaks to the right angles.

Fact: a helmet can save your life

I've definitely had my life saved by a helmet. Not necessarily through crashing – although who can say to what extent a helmet saved me during my crash in Monaco qualifying 2003 – more through strikes. I've had bits of metal hit my helmet, and on one particular occasion very early in my career I was testing with Williams in South Africa, hurtling down the back straight when a bird hit me. It didn't dent the helmet but it scratched the visor and it did my neck in.

'I've hit a bird,' I yelled over the talkback.

'You shouldn't do that, young man,' came the reply (different times, different times…).

I was a bit sore afterwards and I had bits of bird dribbling down my visor, which was fairly upsetting, and of course I felt terrible for the poor old bird whose death was the very definition of being in the wrong place at the wrong time. But I was alive, which was the main thing.

Years later, at Brawn, there was a terrible incident during qualifying at the 2009 Hungarian Grand Prix where part of the suspension came off Rubens' Brawn and struck Felipe Massa in the Ferrari on his helmet, just an inch above the eye and knocking him unconscious. The thing was, it went through his visor and gave him a head cut and bone damage to his skull.

He was fine eventually, thank God, but as a result of that accident they introduced a carbon-fibre piece that sat on top of the visor and made it smaller. It was an interim measure before they could introduce a regulation to make the visor slot even smaller, which they did eventually, so the visor slot is tiny.

The helmets we used were made of carbon fibre so not only are they very light – about 2kg – but they're safe, too, which is in fact their primary function: safety. You would be amazed if you picked up a crash helmet how light they are, but also how robust. It brings it home to you when you're driving around and see people on bikes, especially some of the 'biker' type helmets you see, that would be less than useful in a crash and would be better suited to a mantelpiece than your head on a freeway.

The funny thing is that a helmet has to dent on impact otherwise your head takes all the impact, your brain moves and you get brain damage. There has to be some flex in the helmet in order to absorb the impact.

Fact: it makes a driver cross when someone puts his helmet down the wrong way

So say if you're at a photo shoot, suited and booted, you hand your helmet to the PR guy and he plops it down the wrong way up. Not only is there the risk that the paint will get scratched, but it's a respect thing – respect the lid.

Fact: helmets mean a lot to a driver

Obviously, we have no input whatsoever in the livery of the car. Nobody asks a driver what colour they'd like the car or where they think the sponsor logos should go. When it comes to helmets, though, we have most of the input and it's a right and privilege that we guard jealously and treasure because it's the only personal thing that we have. The only thing that we can actually sit down and design ourselves.

Me, I go for a bright colourful design. I've got my Union Jack on the back and it's me all over. Daniel Ricciardo's is always fun, He was sporting a half-pink, half-blue number the last time I saw him, and very fetching it was too.

Daniel's been able to benefit from leaving Red Bull, of course, which is the only team who have any direct input into their drivers' helmets, and then only because they pay them to have the Red Bull logo around it. At McLaren, we had certain parameters, so you had to have a white ring around the helmet for the sponsor's logo but the rest of it was your choice: your colour, your design.

The genesis of my helmet design comes from karting days. In 1994, I was literally handed a helmet with a Union flag on the back and sides, and I liked it so much I used that design – or variations of that design – in karting, Formula Four and Formula Three. It was only when I got to Formula One that a helmet designer at Bell Helmets told me I couldn't copyright the design, which meant that anybody could wear my helmet. And since the whole idea was to create something unique to me, that felt like defeating the purpose.

Instead we came up with the 'JB' design, which looks almost like a Union flag. It did by then anyway, and I thought it was really cool, so that's how the JB started.

A lot of my career was with Bell Helmets, and then the relationship went sour for one reason or another, and so I started working with Arai helmets, who were like, 'Why don't we change the design a bit?' And I began with this guy, Uffe Tagström, a Finnish guy who also designs Kimi's helmets, and what he did was to integrate the JB flag design, along with a little Johnnie Walker figure, who were one of the main sponsors, and that was pretty much the basis for all of my helmet hats from then on.

I've changed the colours a few times – I've had red and white; silver, red and white; pink, and the Brawn colours, which is what I have now – and I've added bits to it, so now there are dragons on the back, while at times I had the Ichiban team triathlon logo on the back, and I had a Papa Smurf on the back for a couple of years after the old boy passed away.

The sponsors are painted on if we know we're going to keep them all year, otherwise it's stickers. I'd say we get four or five helmets a year. Well, that's nowadays, in Super GT. But when I was in F1, it was 18 helmets a year, a helmet per race, each of which would be bagged up and put away after the race. I was never superstitious about my helmet. I'd rather have six helmets that each won one race than one that won six, but that might be because I love collecting them, which I think is common to all drivers. I make sure that I hang on to all of my winning helmets so I have all 15 of my wins. Others I've given away to charity, and I've given a fair few to friends and family and there's a bit of swapping that goes on between drivers.

You have to be choosy, mind. I only want to swap helmet hats with certain drivers, and they would be drivers with whom I have some kind of history, either because we were mates off the track, or because we had some great racing on it.

Tearing one off

That time the bird hit me, and I had bits of bird sliding down my visor? That's when I needed the tear-offs, which are removable plastic strips on the top of your visor that you rip off to remove the oil, dirt, bits of rubber and occasional dead bird that you may encounter during the drive. There are four of them, and it's a rare race that you don't use all four. It's designed to make it easy to remove with your gloved hand, so you just reach with your opposite hand, pull it off and then you…

Ah, well, therein lies a tale. Because in ye olden days we'd just toss the used bit of plastic out of the car, but I think it was Valtteri Bottas who threw one out of his and it either went into his airbox, or the airbox of the car behind, and overheated the engine.

No doubt this sport that prides itself on detail and perfection decided that maybe it wasn't the best idea to have random plastic booby traps flying around the track like discarded McDonald's wrappers, and so we were asked to get rid of it in a pocket in the car, which meant that all the teams were testing various sticking pocket things and it was all a bit of a joke. So they've gone back to chucking them out of the car.

Meanwhile, on a car with a roof and a windscreen, the tear-offs will be on the windscreen itself. Big, family-size tear-offs. At Le Mans you have something like 16 tear-offs on the screen and at every pit stop one of the mechanics will lift the wipes, tear off the plastic and suddenly you have a brand-new pristine-clean windscreen. It's ace.

In motocross they have one on a reel on the helmet visor, which sounds like a good idea, because at least you don't gets bits of plastic flying around, and after all, it's that bit better for the environment. But I guess in Formula One it would be (official reason) aerodynamically inefficient and (unofficial reason) just not cool enough.

Meanwhile, I'm often asked if I'd be buried with my helmet hat and the answer is no – because I'll probably be cremated. But it's certainly true that if you see the funeral of a driver, you generally see their helmet on a stand. You might wonder if it's in bad taste, especially if the driver died racing. After all, the helmet didn't save them. But I don't think it matters, really. It's more about the symbolism. The fact that they died doing something they loved, and that being a racing driver was very much a part of their identity.

As for me, the helmet I'd take with me to the afterlife would be my 2009 Monaco-winning helmet. It's the only helmet I've got stored in a Perspex case, and is one of two helmets that are supremely precious to me. That's because it was such a special race. I'd gone into it as Championship leader, not done as well as hoped in practice, and in qualifying was trailing Rubens and Sebastian. Until I put in a late lap – *the* lap, the lap that I'm still likely to say is my favourite-ever, depending on when I'm asked and how I'm feeling at the time – which put me on pole.

After that, I won the race only to park in the wrong place, which meant I had to run down to the podium. And then I partied with Prince Albert at the after-race knees-up, and then on Monday we invented Super Monday. Special, special, special.

The other helmet is the one I was wearing in Brazil that same year, when we actually clinched the World title.

Overalls

We used to have baggier overalls with pockets in them and a Velcro belt. You'd do a photo shoot and have your hands in your pockets looking like something out of the Littlewoods catalogue.

I'm taking the piss but I liked that, actually. I liked the fact that you had something to do with your hands. Here I am standing looking out over Monaco harbour, what should I do with my hands? Oh, I know, I'll store them in this handily placed pocket.

Other than that you don't really need a pocket. I'm sure in the days of James Hunt and Co. they required pockets for a packet of 20 Embassy and a gold-plated Ronson lighter, but these days there isn't quite the need, and with the emphasis on keeping things lightweight, they've got rid of the pockets, and the Velcro belt has gone, too.

I'm not so bothered about the Velcro belt but I do mourn the demise of the pockets. I think that removing the pockets has made the job of looking cool in overalls – which is, after all, a driver's primary role – that bit harder.

At least we're all the same now. The worst thing was that it was one of those marginal gains (more of which later) that took a while to catch on. We at McLaren lost our pockets early doors, but not everybody did. Other drivers would see you coming in the paddock and deliberately put their hands in their pockets, *openly mocking you.* I think most people are the same nowadays, thank God, but it was tough.

Obviously, your suit is plastered with sponsors' logos. But so is your underwear, so that if you unzip the top bit of your overalls there are more logos underneath, like a Russian doll. Mind you, it's frowned upon, unzipping your overalls. The teams like you to keep the overalls zipped up, ostensibly because it's smarter but who wants to bet that it's really to do with sponsorship. We prefer to unzip them, though. Firstly, because they can get a bit hot, and secondly because zipped up they don't leave a lot to the imagination.

4. THE NOT-SO-GREAT AND SOMETIMES DOWNRIGHT YUCKY SHIT

The fear

Yup. It happens. It really does. I remember my second-to-last race in 2016. Brazil, it was, the penultimate race of the season – the race before Abu Dhabi, at which I was due to retire.

It was wet, which should have been perfect conditions for me, and one of those races that I could wring the neck out of and maybe do a little better than expected. I certainly hoped to beat my teammate at the time, who was Fernando.

Turn one, it hit me. I had a bit of wobble, figuratively and literally. The circuit was treacherous with rain and I was sliding all over the place. This was the race I mentioned earlier, where Max Verstappen really showed his skills in the wet. Well, as he was doing that up front, muggins here, the former wet-race specialist, was sliding all over the place at the back, feeling very much not in control of his car, desperately trying and failing to find grip, and feeling...

Fearful.

For the first time ever, I was scared.

I didn't tell anyone at the time. I've hardly told a soul since. But I suffered a loss of nerve that day. It was because I knew I was retiring, and as a result all I could think about was hurting myself. The race was super wet, a tough circuit that even though it had been so good to me over the years was still a dangerous one.

This is not something you'd normally think about. Usually, in fact, you're not thinking in those terms at all. I'll talk about distractions in a bit but I can save you the bother of reading that section by saying that you don't let *anything* distract you when you're driving. It's not a case of having to consciously banish distractions. They simply don't occur to you. You're a driving machine and that's it.

But here I was, *thinking*. I was thinking, *There are two races to go. I don't want to hurt myself. Not when I've achieved so much, come so far.*

I was scaring myself, that was the problem. My head was not in the right place, and I think that's probably the most dangerous scenario. You tense up, and when you tense up like that it's so easy for the car to snap. A bit of oversteer, a bit of understeer, it just goes. You might be going through a corner, hit a river, and if you snatch at the steering you lose grip and it's bang, gone, you're in the wall at 150mph. I didn't want to finish my career like that, or possibly not walk away from something. Ask me my scariest moment in a race car and that was it.

And here's the kicker. Because it was a wet race I was finding it tough to drive the car, which was exacerbating the psychological issue, which made it even harder to drive the car, and because of that I couldn't get heat in the tyres, and because of that it made the driving more difficult, which in turn made the psychological issue worse.

As soon as you get tyre temperature in the wet, things get easier, you can start pushing the car and taking risks, but I couldn't even get to that stage.

It's not uncommon. I've heard it said by other drivers that the fear kicks in once you decide to retire. For that reason I think it would be better if you decided, announced and did it all in one go, but of course it can never work like that for many reasons.

Of those who finished, I came last. Fernando, miles in front, was over a second faster than me. I was embarrassed with my performance; I was gutted. Coming in and seeing the team, was the most embarrassing to me. Crashing: shit happens, you say sorry. But to put in such a lacklustre performance was just mortifying. I didn't tell them that I was scared. I just said I didn't turn the tyres on, which I couldn't, because I didn't drive fast enough to turn the tyres on. I don't mind saying that I don't think anyone's better than me in those conditions, but that day, nobody was worse than me. All I could think was that a year ago I would have destroyed that race.

Nerves

Not to be confused with the above, but I do also struggle with nerves, excitement and adrenalin – it all comes at once. How do I deal with it? I don't think I do. I think I just breathe and tell myself, *You've got this. You know what you're doing.*

It's the same with anything I do: triathlons, racing, presenting. And I think it's because you care. That's why you get nervous. Which means, of course, that it's a good thing to get nervous: it's because you care about what you're doing. It also means that when you do achieve something it's going to mean so much more to you.

For that reason I'd never want to get rid of my nerves completely, even if I could; they help you feel present in the moment, they're how you understand that you're doing something different and special. You should nurture and treasure them, not fear them.

That's the difficulty for some people, I think. They let nerves get in the way of Doing Cool Stuff. They don't do the stuff because they're too nervous about it.

Me, I get nervous. No doubt. If it's something worth doing I get nervous. And I also know that the only way to get over your nerves about something is to do it. I mean, it would be so easy to go through life and not be nervous, but that would mean never being out of your comfort zone, and then how would you get the best out of yourself?

I do speeches onstage and in the first 30 seconds I can hear the trepidation in my voice. You might make a little slip-up or rush the answer to something. I say to myself, why the hell are you nervous? Just relax, breathe, take your time,

Thing is, though, although I say that to myself every time, it doesn't really get better.

Panic attacks, fainting and other stuff I'd never have admitted to while in Formula One

I nearly had a panic attack while driving once. It was in 2004, the first-ever Chinese Grand Prix. It was, and still is, hosted at the Shanghai International Circuit where there are four corners where the G-force is so intense that you can't breathe.

Fair play, I was warned. My engineer said, 'You probably won't breathe on those four corners, because the G-force is five-plus' like it was nothing.

I was like, *Really? Come on...* And then I went out, tried to breathe, couldn't breathe, and got a bit... well, worried. Not panicked. That tale is to come. But certainly more than slightly concerned, a feeling that was characterised by a sense of incredible claustrophobia. I didn't faint, though, thank God, because driving a car around the circuit in China is not a time you want to be fainting.

The panic, though. That was another time. In 2014 I was fitness training someplace overseas that I won't name for reasons that will shortly become clear. Perhaps training a little too hard, I developed quite serious back pain. So bad that I couldn't walk, and if I lay down I couldn't get up.

So I took myself off to this little sports clinic they had in the hotel, where the nurse took a look and said, 'Right, we're going to give you an injection.'

'Where?' I said.

'In here,' she said.

'No,' I said, 'whereabouts on the body?'

'Oh,' she said, 'it's in the bum.'

'Okay,' I said, and assumed the position.

In went the needle, and I can only assume she got it wrong. Well, *something* went wrong anyway, because all of a sudden I was in very serious pain.

And I mean big pain. Proper searing agony.

'I'm going to faint,' I managed. 'I'm going to faint, I'm going to faint,' and she removed the needle but by then it was too late and I had indeed lost consciousness.

My companion at the time said I had gone white and then purple and that I'd stopped breathing. I remember coming round and finding myself in a weird state of suspension between conscious and unconscious. I could hear things. I could hear people talking in the room. But I wasn't there with them yet. It was as though I was underwater and very slowly moving towards a light-dappled surface.

When I eventually opened my eyes, I was even more confused and that gave me a moment of full-on, almost-losing-the-plot panic, which I'm pretty sure is the only time I've ever properly panicked in my life. All I can say is that when it comes to panic you know it when you feel it, and I certainly felt it then.

Still, I left it there in the clinic – or thought I had.

Then, about five months later, it happened on a plane. Suddenly I felt terribly claustrophobic. It wasn't as though I felt trapped on the plane. Maybe a bit. But it was more that I was trapped inside my own body. Gripped by an overwhelming urge to get out.

I had a word with myself. Got through it. Feeling very rattled about it, though, I took myself off to the doctor. He gave me an X-ray.

'Well,' he said, 'there's nothing wrong with you.'

'Are you sure?' I said, squinting at the X-rays in search of strange shadows or bits of shrapnel.

He said, 'I'm sure it's a mental thing. We can give you some drugs to sort it out, but to be honest it's something you've got to deal with on your own. It might be tough and it might be freaky at times, but you've got to try and get a handle on it.'

It's a type of anxiety, he added. According to him it's like a brain fart (my terminology, not his). It's when you're not doing anything and your brain goes into a kind of zombie slumber state. It's like a form of accidental meditation. Then, when your brain kicks into gear, it feels as though it's behind your body.

'That's the feeling you're having,' he told me. 'It's your brain trying to play catch up.'

And he was right that getting a handle on it is very much something that I've had to sort out myself. Sure enough, I've found myself in a situation in which I'm struggling, like being on a plane or in a confined space, I sort of flash back to that moment in the hotel sports clinic, and I can sense a residual feeling of panic wanting to return. At these times I have to be careful to manage it, not let it find its full expression.

It's no longer an issue because I've learnt to control it, which is mainly down to controlling my breathing. Or, rather it was about remembering to breathe, because that, essentially, was the problem: I was not remembering to breathe.

Like I say, I told no one. This is because, a.) if you tell someone that makes it A Thing, and I didn't want to give it that lofty status, b.) I'm British and we tend not to discuss that sort of thing, preferring to drink tea, slice cucumber for our sandwiches and address the important subject of the weather, and c.) I'm a Formula One driver and if there any chinks in our armour we cover them up; we do our best to hide them, because our rivals certainly won't be revealing their frailties any time soon.

Because I was still racing in F1 I'd occasionally get this feeling while at work. I remember being on the massage couch with Mikey working on me, and having to get up and walk outside. I told him that I needed some fresh air, and I did, although I knew there was more to it than that.

Sure enough, outside in the fresh air I felt no better. I was still thinking, *I feel like I'm going to faint. (Only I know I'm not going to faint, it's just that breathing thing again.) Except I think I'm going to faint.* Which, of course, brings a whole new level of anxiety, in turn worsening the fear of fainting.

I got there, though. As with other times. I overcame the feeling by remembering to breathe and relax. You're thinking, *Yeah, easy.* It's not. It took me over a year to get a handle on that little lot.

'We don't talk about crashes'

It's true. We talk about 'issues in the race'. You know, if you get a puncture on the rear, you have to close and thus lock the differential or risk damage because one wheel's turning a lot faster than the other. If you break a front wing, you need to let us know before you come into the pits. Things like that. Never *If you have a crash and think your leg's fallen off, this is what to do.*

What we did have, however, was a procedure for quick extraction out of the car. This came via an FIA ruling, which said that you can't race unless you can get out of the car and put both feet on the floor in five seconds flat.

It became a bit of a competition. The FIA steward would get to you and he'd been to five teams already and you're, like, 'What's the time to beat?'

He'd be, 'Well, Vettel did it in three point seven.'

So you're, 'Okay, let's try and beat it.'

You'd do it. 'Go on then,' you'd say, 'what was my time?'

'You did it in three point nine. Well done, you passed…'

'Wait, wait, wait. Where do you think you're going? Let me have another go…'

And you'd do it in three point five. And your knees are sore and you've done your back in, but it was worth it knowing that you've won.

Another thing: we were told not to exit the car until we were informed that it's safe. Teams can tell from sensors on the car what sort of G the driver has pulled in the crash and if you've pulled 35G, which is the limit for possible distortion to the neck, you'll need to wait for the all-clear to get out.

So if your car catches fire, say, you get out in your five seconds. If you crash, though, and it's a crash at speed, you have to wait to hear, and it may well be that you'll need to be seen by medics and attended to by FIA stewards who will extract you from the car still strapped into your seat so that your neck doesn't move (the in-car rig that allows this was introduced to the sport by the late, great Sid Watkins, the neurosurgeon who probably did more to improve safety in the sport than anybody else). They can do this in about four minutes flat. They help you out, in the seat, having spoken to you first ensure that you've replied to them in the correct manner and then they take you out.

Crashing is a disappointment, of course, but I've never been upset with the team for something breaking, ever, even when I've had suspension failure and hit the barriers really hard in testing, which is a horrible feeling. The air is sucked out of your lungs, you've got nothing in you any more. It's just that feeling of being winded. The worst, most horrible feeling.

Not only that, but if you hit a tyre barrier at speed you're never sure if you're going to come out the other side. It doesn't matter how hard you hit it, you can always see the worst.

The real scary stuff is the car stopping so quickly, like when it hits something, because that's when you pull the high G and your brain moves in your skull and you either get brain or neck damage or you're dead. When you see a race car rolling it looks really bad, but of the 'bad' crashes it's one of the safest, because you've got your roll protection, you're wearing your helmet hat and the roll action is taking the sting out of the stopping.

The first race that Brittny attended was the opening race of 2016 in Melbourne, when Fernando Alonso had a nasty crash. Got airborne, rolled it into a wall. But he got out. He was dazed, but okay because he didn't hit anything hard, because although he came to rest against the wall, it wasn't like he 'hit' it . You look at the crash, it looks bad. Just the state of his car afterwards. It looks like it's been through the crusher. You might even think it looks worse than me hitting the wall at Monaco in 2003. But of the two mine was potentially much worse, because of the sudden stop.

And I bet any money he went back to look at that accident on YouTube, because it's a fact of life that you can't help but feel proud of a crash like that; you watch it and you think, *I got out of that.*

With all drivers, especially younger drivers, if they have a big shunt and it scares them, you need to put them in a car straightaway. If they have a week to think about it they might not be the same ever again. So, you've got to get them over it immediately. I know it's an old-school way of doing it, but it works.

As far as I'm concerned – and apart from *that* situation – I've never really been fearful in Formula One. It is, after all, a very safe sport, despite the obvious dangers. I guess that as a racer I take more risks in my life than a lot of people but I don't tend to worry about myself as much as I worry about family and friends driving. As a family we often used to go indoor karting, and I remember feeling very anxious watching my dad and sisters tearing around the track. I didn't enjoy it as much as I should have done for that reason.

Extend that feeling and I can understand why, as a parent, it must be tough seeing your kid race knowing that he could get hurt. I can understand how my mum didn't like it at first. Maybe never really got used to it. Sorry, Mum.

The bodily functions

Sometimes you can get in the car a bit early, feel like you're dozing off and get an erection. Look, it happens, okay? Why do you think they call it a cockpit?

Farting's great because it stays in the cockpit. I'd always call my mechanic over. 'Mate, can I ask you something?' and he'd put his head in the cockpit and know instantly. 'Aw, you dirty bastard' and then I'd hold his arms so he couldn't get away.

I'm telling you, this is what passes for sophisticated humour in a Formula One garage.

I've never done a wee in the car, because I think it's disgusting. (Whereas farting on your mechanic's head is fine. That, in fact, is exactly where I draw the line.) I know that drivers have done it, though, and I'm sure it couldn't be avoided but I still wonder how it happens, because if you're managing your hydration correctly, then you should have drunk exactly the right amount. What's more, you should be sipping it, and as you know, if you sip a drink you don't wee as much; it's when you drink in gulps that it goes right through you. These are the things you have to learn as an F1 driver: don't gulp, sip.

Other occupational hazards

When I started in F1, I got sick a lot, often when I turned up at tests. As a result, teams thought that I was trying to get out of testing the car, which is a fairly ridiculous notion, given that I lived and breathed racing. Why on earth would I *not* want to test the car?

So anyway, I'd say, 'No, trust me, I am ill', and I'd be in my hotel room feeling totally crock. It was the physio of the team who told me, 'You can only drink rice water.'

I was like, 'You what?'

It's true. It's a thing. Basically when they boil rice, they take the rice out and give you the water to drink, so what you get is a cup of insanely starchy water. And the brilliant thing is, it works: it helps you hydrate and helps everything stick together. You stop feeling so nauseous.

And then you're put on solids, which would be rice or pasta with no sauce, something very bland, before they might let you have some proper, grown-up food.

I don't get that problem any more. I think it's because the standard of food across the board has improved so much, nowhere more so than on flights. Or maybe it was simply a case of me, a bloke from Somerset, adjusting to the life of a globe-trotting sex symbol. My constitution couldn't quite handle it.

Other things: your neck goes. F1 drivers tend to have very pronounced neck muscles as well as greater-than-usual incidences of sore neck simply because there's so much pressure on your neck. Coming in from the drive, you'll be getting out of the car and just feel it go. It just goes solid. So you have to watch for that.

What else? I've had cramping in my leg before from the brake pedal. I've had a couple of cars where the master cylinder of the brakes is bigger, meaning the brake pedal's even firmer and then you've got to hit the pedal even harder, making it almost undriveable at Monza. I'm not joking. At the end of an hour and a half, your leg is ready to give up.

I'll tell you something else that racing drivers are especially susceptible to, and it's not just dry skin, although that definitely is one, it's wrinkles. Again, I'm not kidding. Put your hands to your face and now drag the skin downwards. That's your skin

when you're wearing a helmet. Add that to the dry skin issue –
which is a result of all the travel – and it's wrinkle city in there.

FINDING
AN EDGE

1. PEAK CONDITION

Reactions, eyesight

Something that we all need as drivers is good hand-to-eye co-ordination. For that you need the BATAK wall. It's like a very big and sophisticated version of the old Simon Says game, where you have to hit the lights as they come on. So it's testing and improving your reaction times as well as working on your peripheral vision, because the idea is that you're supposed to just stare straight in front and rely on your peripheral vision to see the outer lights, which is good for drivers.

Most drivers have better than 20/20 vision. I don't know what's better than 20/20 vision: '20/20 vision plus', I guess. They say my eyesight is as good as it ever was, but I'm not so sure. If I'm looking at a timing screen in a race, it's not quite as clear as it used to be. Time will tell, I suppose.

Diet, fitness

Told you we'd get here. These days the younger drivers are taught the doctrine of good diet and fitness from the year dot. Whether they take any notice of it is up to them, and perhaps if they're already the right size and shape for a racing driver (e.g., small) then they can get away with being a bit relaxed on that front.

The rest of us? Ah, not so much. I fell slightly between the generations: too old for the incomers who are taught the benefit of nutrition and exercise and provided with all the support they need to make the most of the advice they're given; too young to be a fully paid-up member of the Watney's Red Barrel brigade.

I was one of those who pretty much had to find out for myself. I'm not going to say that I was in the vanguard of a new way of thinking in Formula One, leading the charge, changing things from within. No. I'm going to leave you to come to that conclusion by yourself.

Neither am I for one second ragging on any of the generations that came before me. No way. I've driven an F1 car from back in the 1970s and I can tell you that fitness came a distant second to bravery where the drivers were concerned. Those things were dangerous. Drivers were surrounded by petrol tanks. One spark and the lot goes up in an inferno. They're awkward to drive, too, because they're not built with the driver in mind. It's more like, 'Here's the car, get in and drive it,' so your arms are sticking out at strange angles. You're trying to manage the gear stick. You're trying to not become a human fireball. Frankly, being a fearless contortionist is more important than being fit.

So the cars changed, and of course drivers had to adapt. I'd be interested to see a graph of the increased neck musculature in the average Formula One driver versus the increase in G-forces across the board. I bet there's an exact correlation. It's probably equally fair to say that as the engineers came up with more aerodynamic cars the G-forces increased, it took drivers a while to latch onto the fact that they needed to up their game.

Back in the day, nobody was promoting fitness. It was just me and Mark Webber pretty much. Nowadays, every driver's posting and I think for many different reasons: one, because they need to train; two, because it looks good on social media and reflects well on them; three, because the team sees them working hard and focusing on their job.

This last is an important consideration, because when the driver's away from the team, the team doesn't know what the driver's doing. Are they just partying or are they actually working on trying to make themselves a better racing driver? Oh look there's a social media post of him doing some star jumps. What a good boy.

But why do you need to be fit, you ask, when all you're doing is driving? Well, we've already talked about the effort involved in braking. You can't run the power steering too high either, because you lose feeling from the car. Personally, I like to run the power steering low, because I want to feel more through the car. Another reason is the high-frequency vibration you're subject to. They try and dampen it (because it's bad for the car, not because they care about you) but even so, you still have a lot of high-frequency vibrations while driving, which for the driver gets very tiring because of the build-up of lactic acid, which is wearing for your muscles and mentally draining as well.

Being fit is the best way to quickly disperse lactic acid in your body. That and staying hydrated by putting in the right fluids into your body, the right salts and minerals.

For me, another way to help with it was to cycle, because cycling on the roads in the UK, you get a lot of vibrations and that builds up a lot of lactic acid and it's how your body deals with the issue.

Added to all of that, you need high levels of fitness to withstand the huge amount of G-force you're subjected to in high-speed corners.

A further thing you have to bear in mind in terms of withstanding G is your weight. For drivers like me who are tall, it's a difficult balance because we have to be fit, we have to be strong, and we have to have good cardiovascular fitness.

But we also had to be the weight of a jockey.

So me, I'm super-light for someone who's six foot tall, just 6 per cent body fat, which is at the very lower end of the 'athlete' scale (the 'average' is 18–24 per cent body fat), but I also had to be muscular as well because I had to have the strength to drive the car.

It used to be the case that the weight of the car and the driver were considered together, and that to bring the package up to the minimum weight requirement, teams could make up the shortfall by adding ballast to the car and thus optimise its balance. Clearly this gave an advantage to the shorter and/or skinnier drivers, especially when you consider the calculation that 10kg of extra weight on a driver translates to three-tenths of a second lap time, which in our world is longer than sitting through all three *Godfather* movies.

However, the regulations in F1 have changed so the minimum weight for a driver is 80kg now and if you're only 65kg, you have to ballast up, and that ballast has to go in the cockpit, not elsewhere in the car, so you no longer benefit from being skinny. But when I was racing, if you were light you were light, and if you were heavy then you were heavy, and the latter would really hurt you because the car would be overweight.

So it was a big deal. Some of the guys were starving themselves. Drivers like Nico Hülkenberg and Adrian Sutil, who were even taller than me, were just skin and bones. So we had a drivers' meeting where the majority agreed that it was wrong. It shouldn't be like this. And Felipe Massa, who was probably the shortest driver and definitely one of the lightest, piped up and said, 'No, it's the rules, it's what it is.'

We were, like, *Are you kidding?* He was gaining lap time simply because he's 20kg lighter than some of the drivers. *How could you be like that? How can you want to win like that?*

'Well, it's the regulations, isn't it?'

'Well, that's why we're trying to change it.'

He never understood how bad he looked by saying that. It never occurred to him to wonder why nobody else agreed with him. And the reason that nobody else agreed with him was because we all believed it should be a level playing field. Let the talent, let the cars do the talking, not how good you are at saying no to cream cakes. Very strange.

So to diet, and at McLaren we had the late Dr Aki Hintsa to advise on nutrition. I went to Finland to spend some time with him where we went cross-country skiing and he helped me with my diet, especially regarding my post-training nutrition. Below is the way I roll if I'm training, say to get in shape for racing, or for a triathlon.

Typical Menu

A man should be eating 2,500 calories without doing any fitness at all. Me, I've got a very fast metabolism. I can eat a lot of ice cream, for example, and get away with it. Yeah, all right. Don't hate me.

Breakfast

In the morning, pre-training, I find it difficult to get enough calories in my system, so to start with I would have porridge with berries and almond milk to give me more calories, not just water, and maybe some granola and chia seeds on top as well. So that would be my start to the day, which is about 500 calories.

Post-breakfast

I'd train for a couple of hours on a bike, eating every hour, obviously hydrating the whole time. You're supposed to do a bottle an hour of liquid – 750mgs – although I probably didn't do quite as much as I should, maybe more like 500mgs.

At the end of the ride, I'd have a protein shake with carbohydrates in powder form, about 300 calories.. This doesn't taste of anything, it just adds to the carbohydrates that you need post-training.

If you're doing a severe training session then you maybe need more carbs. You don't need it if you're doing a 30-minute run or a high heart-rate run. It's the long stuff that you really need to get the carbohydrates in for a run of an hour or longer, or a cycle ride of two-and-a-half, three hours. That was my biggest issue: I couldn't get enough carbohydrates in, but I didn't want to eat sugar, because sugar deposits as fat, and you get a massive peak and then you drop.

Lunch

I would eat lunch as soon as I could after training, which would be high in protein, Normally, it would be either fish or chicken, usually chicken, as well as trying to get the greens in, up to about 700 calories.

Post-lunch

In the afternoon, I'd do an hour-and-a-half swim, or go for an hour run. Straight after that a protein shake again, so about 300 calories, I guess.

Dinner

Again, protein. It sounds like a hell of a lot of food, but you've got to think how much you're burning doing those activities. I was doing three to four hours a day, and even though I was eating that much I'd still struggle to get the enough food, especially enough carbs in. How would I know if I wasn't getting enough carbs? My recovery would suffer. The next day I'd get up and I'd be in bits; I wouldn't be able to train. So I knew I wasn't getting enough energy into my system to refuel the muscles.

All this is what I learnt initially from Dr Aki. How you have to supplement your fitness with the right food and enough recovery time, and if you don't do that, you get less fit.

Mind you, I still got it wrong. Training for triathlons in 2017, I was pushing myself too hard, not getting enough rest and probably not putting enough food into my body, so I was just getting less and less fit until it was just too much and every time I trained I was weak.

I remember going to see a specialist in Monaco. He was doing all the fat checks and everything.

He said, 'You're twelve per cent fat.'

I was like, 'What? All the training I do?'

He said, '*Oui, vous* is putting *beaucoup de* carbohydrates into *votre* body you don't need.'

'Well, what do I do?'

He said, '*Pas de carbohydrates pour le* breakfast.'

Which translates as no carbs at breakfast.

I was, like, 'But isn't that the time you *should* eat carbo-hydrates? Aren't they fuel that you can use during the day?'

He said, '*Non*. If you eat them at breakfast, *votre* body's going to crave them *pour le* rest of the day. It's all to do with your insulin spiking.' He said, 'I promise *vous*, in two weeks that if you don't eat carbohydrates *pour* le breakfast and instead of eating pasta at lunch eat sweet potato or brown rice you will lose a significant amount of fat.'

'Okay,' I said,

So I did as he said and went back two weeks later: 6 per cent body fat. I'd lost 6 per cent body fat by not eating carbohydrates for breakfast and not eating pasta at lunch but eating brown rice or sweet potato instead.

'Well done, *vous*,' he said.

Hydration

A driver will lose about three litres of fluid during a race. As you can appreciate, then, you need to stay hydrated and you need to do it right or you will undoubtedly struggle with dehydra-tion. (And this is why I get surprised when I hear about drivers needing a wee on the car.)

At McLaren, I spent quite a lot of time with GSK, GlaxoSmith-Kline, who were the team sponsor. I went to their offices and their sports facility in London, which was great fun. I gave them a rundown of my training schedule and told them what I eat during the day. They did all the tests to tell me where I was in my fitness and where I should be, how much carbohydrates I should be eating, how much protein and so on.

'Your carb intake is good,' they said, 'but you're a little bit high in fat. You need to cut down on your fat and make sure that the fat you have is from nuts rather than animal fat.'

On my next visit I met the Brownlee brothers, triathlete Olympic Champions Johnny and Alistair, and what GSK did was to pit me against them: we did strength-training comparisons, and then they put us all on bikes, monitored our perspiration, heart rate and so on.

I was against Johnny for that one, and I caught him looking across at me and realised that he was nervous. I was like, 'Mate, you're an Olympic athlete, you're going to kick my arse.'

But he said, 'You're not sweating, you look so relaxed.'

So we did the test, the results came in, and mine were good, but obviously not on the same level as his.

Then we did reaction tests and I destroyed them as I expected to, even though I'm older, because that's part of my job, and really the only area where I'd expect to better them.

GSK also did caffeine tests. How much caffeine should I have before the race? I did six separate goes in the simulator. The first day there was no caffeine at all, the second day they gave me tablets to take, did a reaction test, jumped in, did the simulator, got out, did a reaction test.

The next time was, like, three tablets of caffeine and so on, until it went up so much that by the sixth day I was wide-eyed and shaking and they realised that it was too high. Literally, *high*.

What they worked out was that for me the perfect amount of caffeine is like a double espresso before a race, which is 150mgs of caffeine. Well, that should have been okay, but I started doing it, and I remember my foot bouncing on the throttle pedal through corners, I was that jittery. I can only assume that the boffins at GSK somehow forgot to factor in the adrenalin, or didn't make enough allowance for it.

Aside from that, though, it was a great experience with GSK, and I really enjoyed working hard on those areas. For me, it was an area where I thought no one's better than me. You may have pockets in your overalls, but you won't beat me on diet and fitness.

The day my favourite button broke

GSK also did all the tests for my salt levels in order to determine how much I should hydrate over a race weekend. They do salt checks, to see how much salt you lose in your sweat, and used those findings to create a special saline solution just for me and Lewis. This is the solution we have in the car that's fed to you via a straw that comes up through the helmet, and is dispensed via a button on the wheel.

I'm not sure if it's an apocryphal tale that NASA spent millions developing a pen that would work in space and the Russians just used a pencil. But there's a similar irony at work when it comes to our fluid-dispensing button. Really, it would be easier to suck. Why we don't just suck I have no idea. Possibly it's thought to be a marginal gain. Maybe it's the fact that the fluid-dispensing button is every driver's favourite button and who wants to get rid of that particular comfort blanket?

To be honest, though, sucking would be easier, especially as the button can be a bit fearsome, fire out more quickly than you're expecting (every time – gets you every bloody time) hits you in the back of the throat and makes you cough up saline solution onto the inside of your visor.

Furthermore, what happens if the little motor that powers the fluid-dispensing gizmo breaks? What then?

I'll tell you, because it happened to me in Malaysia in 2001. It was 33 degrees that year. I was jabbing the button, expecting to feel the refreshing and ultimately life-giving burst of liquid into my throat – only nothing was happening.

Kept jabbing in the hope that it was a temporary fault, that the motor was going to kick back into life, but it didn't. Well, the race is an hour and a half and I didn't drink at all. I'd hydrated beforehand, of course, but probably not sufficiently, and anyway, I only drank water in those days. This was before the era of the saline solution.

About 45 minutes into the race, I started shivering. I was feeling cold, even though the ambient temperature was 33 degrees. After about an hour and fifteen minutes, my eyesight began to blur.

'Er, guys…' I began, and told them what was happening.

'JB, just try and relax as much as you can,' was their sage advice.

Either it's a savage indictment of the sport's cavalier attitude to health and safety, or a measure of our total and utter commitment that it didn't occur to any of us that I should pit for water, or even waste five seconds taking on water during a pit stop. And the fact was that I overcame my sickness and I finished the race but, oh my God, I felt so bad that evening. I didn't sleep, I felt so sick. I was drinking as much as I could all night but I was still destroyed. It was worse than any triathlon I've ever done. Everything gets affected. Going to the toilet is horrible. It doesn't come out the way it should. You get headaches, dizziness and sickness. You feel sick, you're spaced out. It's the worst feeling. I wouldn't wish that on anyone.

2. MARGINAL GAINS

The idea of marginal gains came from the Sky cycling team, although I think that was more in the sense that they put a name to something we'd been doing anyway, because one thing Formula One has always been pretty good at is detail. Sports that deal in tenths of seconds tend to be.

So what are marginal gains? They're the little things that when you add them all up add up to something greater. There's a famous story that in 1934 Mercedes scraped the white paint off their car to save weight, giving birth to their silver livery.

Well, that was what you'd call a marginal gain – decades before the term was coined.

These days it can be anything. At one end of the scale it's the sensors – over 100 of them – that we have all over the car. They measure stress and downforce, brake temperature, tyre tread, fuel use, G-force, everything, and this information is fed back to the strategists, every tiny bit of it analysed to see if any setting can be improved.

One quite famous one is the sensors they have on the pit guns so they know the optimum angle for the gun operator to use when he applies the gun to the nut in order to loosen it faster.

We're talking a fraction of a second here – but that's what marginal gains is all about: it's hundreds, maybe thousands of tiny changes that taken together all add up.

Remember the marbles we were talking about? The little bits of waste rubber that flick off the tyre. Sometimes this rubber would sit on a part of the car where they might affect the aerodynamics, so teams would oil it up or apply a special glaze on it so that the rubber would fly off so that you wouldn't lose any downforce. They worked very hard on making sure that the car was seamless. Everything should fit together absolutely perfectly, any seam should be taped. They worked incredibly hard on making sure that gear shifts were as smooth as possible. Normally in a race car the shift is so short that there's a jolt, quite an aggressive one, but we worked out that those shifts were costing us 0.008 second per shift, so they made them seamless. For the driver it wasn't great; you'd be driving and not feel it shifting, no jolt whatsoever, but the trade-off was the gain, and we were always working on that. Always trying to be quicker.

We'd always be trying to make sure the car was as light as possible. So not only did you used to have drivers starving themselves, and they took away our Velcro belt and even our pockets (sniff), but they took a closer look at the overalls, and what we decided to do was have two suits. There was a 'going out' set, which was the suit we wore to sponsor events, photo shoots and meeting the Queen. These overalls had the beautifully embroidered sponsors' badges sewn on.

Then we had the suits that we raced in, where the sponsors' badges were heat-treated onto the fabric, so that they added no weight to the suit. Next they took the straps off the gloves, which was a weight saving of 20g per glove. Then the boots we wore became shoes. Then the shoelaces in our shoes disappeared.

There were other little tricks, too. You'd often see cars driving off the racing line after the race. That's because they were trying to pick up all the marbles in order to increase the weight of the car because they'd been running underweight, and so after that they'd drive onto the dirt and be picking up all kinds of rocks. You could get a couple of kilos that way.

On second thoughts, I'm not sure if that counts as a marginal gain.

3. KNOWING YOUR ONIONS

It was Benetton's Team Director, Mike Gascoyne, who said to me, 'You're never going to get anywhere unless you have an understanding of the car.'

That was the year 2001, a shocking year for me, as I've already said. But in fact, I'd started my racing career with a not-bad understanding of vehicle basics. In 1995, I'd joined Paul Lemmens' GKS Karting team in Belgium. There, I became teammates with Sophie Kumpen, who was then dating Jos Verstappen and who would go on to have a baby called Max with him and oh God I feel old.

Anyway, staying with Paul and Co. in Belgium we were asked to pay our way by maintaining the karts, which meant building the karts, taking engines out so they could be re-tuned, replacing them.

At first I hated it, because I had no understanding of a racing car or kart. Mechanical engineering was definitely not a strong point of mine. But I learnt so much there that it really helped me later on in life and was to stand me in good stead when I took note of Benetton's not-so-gentle urgings, put the life of a lazy playboy behind me and knuckled down to learning my trade.

I soon discovered that I literally didn't know enough. Understanding what weight transfer does, for example. In my second year in F1 I was braking too gently too early. I was braking early, turning in, getting on the throttle, understeering through the corner, making a right dog's dinner of it.

It was a really shit car but, still, my teammate was doing a better job. Over time, however, when I understood what the car was doing I found out how you get a car to pitch; I gained some understanding of weight transfer and because of this I realised that I was braking too early and not hard enough. It was a hangover from lower formulas where you brake early because you don't want to drop your minimum speed too much, so you brake, carry the speed through the corner and get straight back on the power. Whereas, in F1, it's all about being on power as long as possible, so you brake as late as you can, hammer the brakes, there's so much stopping power, turn the car and then accelerate out of the corner. I didn't understand that and I didn't understand why braking early was an issue until I understood about weight transfer, how when you brake hard that makes the front grip and you can turn the car easier, and then get on the throttle.

It's not just the mechanical side of it; it's also caring about your car. In karting I learnt to have so much more respect for the karts as a result of having put them together myself.

That's not something you do in F1, of course, but it's definitely an ethos that I've carried across. It can be easy to divorce yourself from the human labour that goes into these things, especially when they just appear before you, ready and gleaming. But if you've put them together yourself – and / or if you remember that someone else has put them together and keep that human angle in mind – then you'll find yourself being more considerate of the car. You'll think, *I don't want to crash the car, I don't want to damage the car.*

I've always been like that throughout my career. I will go out of my way to not crash. Obviously, the whole idea of racing is to push your car to the limits, but I would normally build up to it, rather than going too far and coming back.

I remember doing an interview with Alain Prost – as in, I interviewed him – and he had exactly the same philosophy: you didn't want to damage the car, you pushed it to the limit, but crashing was a no-no. He said, I would never normally do a manoeuvre where I thought I'm going to crash, or there's too high a risk.

That was a proper *eureka* moment for me, because he had put into words what I'd always felt. As a kid watching Formula One you were either a fan of Ayrton Senna or Alain Prost, who were two of the greatest rivals the sport has ever seen. Youngsters especially gravitated towards Ayrton – I guess because he had that flair about him and could be very hot-headed. However, I always preferred Prost, the man they nicknamed 'The Professor'. I loved his dedication and his methodical approach. It was like the tortoise and the hare. He wasn't as quick as Ayrton over a lap but over a race he was just as fast – Prost was playing the marginal gains game way before it hit town.

So anyway, to do that interview with my hero and have him articulate exactly the way I felt about driving was a big moment for me. Unconsciously, I'd been emulating him. Not just in his racing style, but also in his whole approach to the sport, because he was definitely one who worked with the team, adapting the car to suit his style.

And to do that, you need to understand it.

I had a chat with another driver a couple of years back. 'How was the car in the race?' I asked him.

He said, 'Yeah, good, it felt good.'

I said, 'Did you do much set-up work before you went out?'

'The team might have done,' he replied, wearing his snapback.

I was, like, 'Really?'

He said, 'I just know I had to drive it really quick. But I don't really know engineering-wise, I just tell them what's wrong and they set it up for me.'

And I think that's quite normal for drivers. The clue is in the job title.

But for some of us, it's important to understand what's wrong, as in, why the car doesn't feel right. It's about finding the right language to explain what's wrong. And that can often come through developing a greater understanding of the machinery.

For example, you have understeer on the turn. They might say, 'Shall we do the front wing?'

In other words: is the problem to do with aerodynamics?

And you go, 'No, it feels like it's more of a mechanical issue, because it's at a lower speed.'

Already you're talking their language. Because you've developed a knowledge of the car you have the confidence to meet them on their turf, and from that you get a proper meeting of minds. Yes, the engineer is the experienced one, he's the one who's educated. Most of these guys went to either Harvard if they went to school in America, or they went to Cambridge or Oxford. But they're not the ones driving. Even if they were allowed in the car they wouldn't be able to go quick enough to give meaningful feedback on how the car performs.

The person who does that is you. You're the only person trusted to give feedback. It's a cool feeling, being The One, but it's also a scary feeling. And being able to give that feedback, being able to understand the car and communicating that to the team is of the utmost importance. That's how you'll give yourself the edge.

HOW TO NOT QUITE, NOT NEARLY, WIN LE MANS

Show me a racing driver who doesn't want to compete at the Le Mans 24-Hour Race, and I'll show you an imposter. Every driver wants to do that race. Speaking for myself, I wanted to win Monaco. I dreamt of winning the Formula One World Championship, and I wanted to race – and, needless to say, win – at Le Mans.

Incidentally, the other race that they say should be on your racing bucket list is the Indy 500, but I'm going to be an iconoclast here and say I have no interest in doing that one.

Reasons: in 2015, Justin Wilson, an excellent driver from the UK, was killed when he was struck by debris from a car that had hit the wall up front. I knew Justin from having competed against him at karting level. What had hit me even harder than that one was the death of another karting competitor, Dan Wheldon. He'd been perhaps my greatest rival during those days, and we'd had some great races together. He lost his life during a race in 2011.

Both of these deaths were a huge shock to the racing community in the UK, where the safety of the sport has been addressed very thoroughly and with great success. The last death in regular

Formula One was Jules Bianchi in 2015, who became the first death since Ayrton Senna in 1994, when he succumbed to injuries sustained during a crash nine months earlier.

So, yes. No Indy for me, thanks. But Le Mans is definitely one I'd love to go back and challenge for the victory. Why? Because it's all about pushing a car to its limit for an *entire day*.

And you really do push it to the limit as well. Two decades ago, they would tell you to take it easy with the car, every gear-shift would be gentle, don't touch the kerbs because it might damage the suspension, be very, very careful with the brakes.

But things have moved on, and these days you just drive flat out, and it's very tough mentally and physically.

To do Le Mans you have to enter the whole World Endurance Championship, but to be honest all anybody cares about is Le Mans, and that's because it's such a mental race. It's super-long (obviously) and the track's an absolute doozy. Even though they've recently added some chicanes, there are a lot of straights, so you go through the first section which is five or six corners, and then you get on to a loooong straight. You sit there, you're reaching up to 230mph.

Then, *bang*. You brake for a chicane, go through the chicane, back on to the same straight. *Bang*. Brake for a chicane, go through that. Back on the straight at 230mph...

It's mostly straights before you get to the last section, the Porsche kerbs, which is a section of high-speed corners. There, you go left, then you go right, double left, right, left, right, left

and that brings you to the end of the lap on what is a phenomenal section.

The race is very fast. There are some slow corners but it's the
fast ones you remember – the ones you take at 160mph, so it's
crazy, and that's just during the daytime. At night it gets even more
mad. You're coming up fast on the slower cars, watching for fatigue
in yourself and in the car. The sheer effort of remaining focused is
exhausting. Which is, of course, a massive part of the appeal.

Don't get me wrong. It's 24 hours so it isn't brilliant racing
action the whole way, but then again, an F1 race is only an hour
and a half long, and that has its boring bits. The point is that we
racing drivers like a challenge. We like down and dirty grass-roots
racing. We like something to be a bit gruelling. As a result, it's
always been a source of fascination. When we were racing in F1,
and Le Mans was on the TV, we'd cluster around to watch before
and after our own race, and everybody had seen the famous Steve
McQueen movie, whose name escapes me.

So anyway, we went there knowing that our team, SMP
Racing and its SMP BR01 car, could not beat any of the Toyotas
competing in their own team, Toyota Gazoo Racing.

Toyota are the Mercedes of that class. They had 1,000 horsepower, we had 700. They had more downforce than us, more
efficiency, more reliability, greater experience; they had hybrid
power so their fuel tank was 35kg and filled up in like two seconds,
whereas our fuel tank was three times the size and took forever to fill
in the pits; their car was four-wheel drive, designed to have forward

motion and power through all four tyres, so they can wheel-spin all four and get the right temperature across the board, meaning they can have all four tyres of the same construction. Whereas with a two-wheel drive, like ours, you don't have that, you have no power going through the front tyres so you can't wheel-spin them. This means you have to change the construction of the tyre, otherwise you can't put enough temperature into the front tyres. They just never work. You're just always sliding around.

Then there were the lights. Toyota had spent masses on developing their lights specifically for Le Mans.

The idea was that they would cover everything, whereas ours were like a couple of weak and flickering candles by comparison. If you were at a standstill you might be fooled into thinking they were decent, but not when you were doing the kind of speeds we were: 160mph through a section where reflective signs kept catching your eye and there wasn't enough light on the road. You could be doing 'only' 160mph, but it would feel like 300mph, simply because you couldn't see where you're going.

So why did I want to go if there was no chance of beating the Toyotas, what with me having such a highly developed competitive streak and everything?

Firstly, because there was always the possibility that although we wouldn't beat the Toyotas we might still get a podium. Also, who knows? The Toyotas might have an issue. Two years previously, a Toyota had been leading the race and with one lap to go had a problem and didn't win.

I also knew that Le Mans was about more than just winning. I knew from watching and from hearing from those who had experienced it first-hand – my mate Chrissy won it in 2007 – that there really is nothing like it in racing. I'd heard that the night-time racing adds a new dimension; that the fans are rabidly enthusiastic and stay up all night, their support never flagging; how the team is exhausted but it's a real group effort; you're all in it together and working as a team.

That last point is important. We drivers get a bit of kip, but the mechanics don't. They work straight through – and not just 24 hours, but 48, because they're building the car the day before, making sure everything's ready for the race – so that by the time the chequered flag is waved they're beside themselves with fatigue. To them it doesn't really matter where you've finished, the fact is that you've finished.

So I wanted to go there and get a feel for it. Yes, my ultimate aim was always to go to Le Mans and win (spoiler alert: it still is) so this was more of a practice to get the experience, thinking that in the future I could take advantage of a rule change and go back with a manufacturer, a lot of whom are likely to be interested in doing Le Mans in 2021 (watch this space).

So to the race itself. The build-up to it you already know. That was me using my mate's simulator, meaning that I was familiar with the circuit – well, a digital version of it at least.

Arriving at the 'Circuit de la Sarthe', aka Le Mans, in the Grand Ouest area of France, we were told the weather for the race was likely to be dry and sunny, and so it proved. Qualifying went well. Our Number 11 SMP Racing car was seventh on the grid behind the two Toyota teams (It Has Started), Rebellion Racing and our sister car, number 17.

We started the race with one of my co-drivers, Vitaly Petrov, at the wheel and had a sensor problem after ten laps, so we had to pit and were in the pits for two hours.

Now, even in a 24-hour race you don't want to be in the pits for two hours. We lost something like 45 laps as a result of being in the pits for that long. It was a race-wrecking, hope-destroying amount of time to be in the pits, and by the time we eventually trundled out again we were last by a long way, knowing that we had another 21 hours of pushing forward in the sure knowledge that our only reward would be to finish.

But…

This was Le Mans. A lot of entrants don't finish. Finishing is good in the context of Le Mans. Finishing well is a bonus. Podium or even – gasp – first, and that's your boyhood racing dream right there. So although you might have been seeing a few heads go down, we battled on.

Mentally, though, it's really tough for a driver. My co-drivers for the race, Vitaly and Mikhail Aleshin, went out and did sterling work, and then it was my turn, and I strapped in and decided to just have fun.

You have cars from several different categories racing at Le Mans, so I was still passing a lot of traffic, which is always good for a boost, plus I was having a great time racing cars from our category. Also, my first drive was from about 6pm when it was still light, so I was driving through sunset and into the night. On the one hand it's a beautiful time of day, but on the other it's a tough bit of the drive to do because the sun's so low in the sky. There's one corner where you're doing 220mph. It's at the end of a straight and there's a little kink, which was easy flat, but with the sun at that height you were blind so you were basically driving by memory of where this kink appeared in the straight.

Now, that's not such a problem if you're on your own, but if there's traffic in front, which there always will be at Le Mans, and it's doing 30mph slower than you, which it often is, then you have a problem, because at a time like that, with a car in front, going by memory isn't really an option.

So that was hard, to say the least. Still, the rest of the circuit was fine. It's a great feeling when the sun goes down and it's pitch black and all the cockpit lights suddenly become really bright and you feel like you're alone. You're looking around and it's so surreal because you're passing a Ferrari, you're 30–40mph quicker and you're towing up behind it, overtaking it, pulling back in. The Le Mans track is just under eight-and-a-half miles long, and it's a mix of dedicated race circuit and normal roads that are open to the public the rest of the year. These sections have a dotted line down the middle and, you know how roads are, they have a camber so the rain runs off. When you pull out to overtake at that speed the car jumps a little to the side, and then when you pull back in, it jumps to the other side again. Even after having driven for so many years, I've never felt that.

It's emotional, too, because it's just you and the car for so long. Together you're dealing with so many different situations. Overtaking traffic, fighting with other cars, feeling your way around a circuit you don't really know that well.

Oh yeah, because it turns out that my mate's simulator hadn't actually prepared me as well as I'd hoped. What's more, I'd only done 12 laps in practice. But in many ways that added to the magic of the occasion. All that crash-course learning was great fun.

My stint was three and-a-quarter hours long, and I was wired when I came into the pits for the changeover.

The first time I did a driver change – in practice, this was – I was like, 'We can't do this – it's too difficult.'

It took us over 45 seconds. You're getting out of the straps. You're trying to clamber out of this tiny space with lots of sharp edges – built for endurance rather than swift driver changes. It's a sort of push–pull movement that you do, and you better be skinny as well, or you're not coming out of that car. Once you're out you literally fall in a heap to the ground.

Oh, and while all this is happening don't forget about your seat spacer, because there's no adjusting the seat in a Le Mans car, it's all done with seat spacers. At the same time the new driver has to put his seat spacer in – all affixed with Velcro, the racer's friend – and then he jumps in.

It's very difficult to get out. You always hit your knees and your shinbones and you basically fall to the floor, so the other driver can jump over you and into the car, because you have 30 seconds to do a full driver change. Not that it really mattered, because we were so far back, but we did it anyway, and we did it in 30 seconds, just.

With that done, I dragged myself to my feet, watched the car go out and then trudged back to the garage surfing a weird mix of emotions. The drive itself had been intoxicating but I was dog-tired. The experience had been incredible, and yet of the cars that had not yet retired, we were last.

At some point, I discovered that our sister car, number 17 – or the number 17 SMP Racing BR Engineering BR1-AER, to give it its full title – had suffered a rear suspension failure and had to leave the race. I think he'd been running in third at the time, so that was a bit gutting. It showed that we had the muscle.

Back in the garage, I ran into Chrissy just as I was taking off my helmet. Bear in mind that Chrissy's known me since the year dot. He looked at me, and the expression he wore was one of complete shock. He was, like, 'Are you okay?'

I went, 'I think so,' and stared at him with wired eyes that were as big as saucers.

'Well, it's just you're white.'

'Okay...'

'Like absolute Persil white.'

I think it was because of the sheer effort of concentrating in the dark

He said, 'I've never seen you look like that. You look like shit.'

Such a charmer. Still, more than anyone, Chrissy knew what racing at Le Mans takes out of you. They don't tell you that. But it does. I was all over the shop. I felt like I'd had five shots of tequila for lunch: tired, disorientated, lurching drunkenly one way and then the other.

The team and Chrissy helped me back to the hospitality area where the first thing I did was start rehydrating, then I took a shower and had a rub down, at which point they began to stretch me out a bit. I could literally feel my muscles uncoil. You're in the same position for three and a half hours in the car, so they need to work on your muscles. It's not like a road car, which is built for comfort, where you have relative freedom of movement. The space is confined. You're frozen pretty much into the same position.

And then you've got to get some food in you, which is the main thing. You'd think that the driver would be ravenous getting out of the car but it's not the case, even though all you've had during the drive is a drink. Just as it is in an F1 car, the drink is dispensed via a button, except – in our car, at least – the drink has a picture of a cocktail glass on it, which is a neat touch. It's a special drink packed with minerals and what have you, and it certainly keeps you going, but it's no substitute for proper food.

Only trouble is, you really have to force that food down. And then you probably have four hours before you're back in the car, maybe a little bit less, and you go off to your little Portakabin where you try and sleep – 'try' being the operative word. The first half an hour, you can't sleep. Your head's spinning. You're still on the circuit.

I remember lying there on a camp bed in a titchy Portakabin unable to believe that I could be so tired – *bone* tired – and yet not fall instantly to sleep. I didn't expect that at all. Finally, I took some melatonin, got to sleep for an hour, woke up to the alarm, thinking, *What the…* and feeling awfully disorientated until the noise of the cars around the track reminded me that I was at Le Mans, and I bounded out of bed.

I took a hot shower, and then I went into the sports area for a massage and some reaction work, firstly on the BATAK wall, and secondly doing an exercise where I'm sitting on a ball having tennis balls thrown at me, catching them while remaining perfectly poised (well, almost) on the ball, the idea being to get back in the game, trying to wake up your unwilling body.

Another snack. By now it was one in the morning and unlike before, the food – fruit and an energy bar – was going down well. Ditto my espresso.

After that I spent about 20 minutes in the garage to get up to speed on current events, watching the car, listening to the driver's comments, chatting to the engineer. At no point did I pay too much attention to the race itself, other than to ascertain that we were still in last. Hey, at least we were still on the track. That, after all, was the important thing. At this rate, we would finish. That, remember, was our aim.

'Put your helmet on, then,' I was told.

And it seemed like only five minutes after I'd got out of the car that I was running out with my helmet on and my seat spacer gripped in one hand, seeing the car coming into the pits and trying to shake off the still spaced-out feeling that was all over me like a winter duvet.

The other driver, Vitaly, jumped out, I hurled my spacer in and climbed in over him, wriggling into position as the straps were fastened over me. They dropped the car, which started up automatically as soon as all four wheels touched the tarmac – pretty cool feature, that – out of the pit lane, and then it was all go again for the next 3 hours, 46 minutes.

This time I felt so much more at home. It was like I'd got the hang of the whole experience. Before I'd had a good time but I still felt I was racing by the seat of my pants; I'm not sure I'd ever felt in control of the whole experience. Now, I was.

Sunrise came, and it was beautiful. Not just the warm glow it cast over the circuit, but the fact that all of a sudden I could see again. For the first time since the previous day, I was able to fully make out the cars I was overtaking, and what a difference it made. I could see that they bore battle scars: ripped-off wheel arches and rubber marks down the side. On some the lights weren't working or hung off at odd angles, having been hit over-night. And every single one was filthy.

What's more, of course, my vision was better and the circuit was still cold. Everything works at that time of day, so the lap times are really fast. I finished my stint, went back, ate, tried to sleep (no joy this time), massage, reaction work, and I was told that my final stint would be the last of the race. 'So you're going to bring the car home.'

'Cool.'

And so now, of course, it was about us finishing. Which is not to say we were taking it easy, because at the end of the day we're racing drivers and there's no point in being out there unless you're pushing it to the max, and so we were.

'Wait, though,' they said.

'What?'

'Well, there's a slight problem with the engine.'

It turned out that they didn't want me to over-rev the engine, so I had to short shift, not using the dull rpm. It was a temperature thing. So they wanted me to shift exactly on the indication lights. Don't delay. Be precise. At the same time there was a guy by the car with a computer plugged in, which is never a good sign. Like Han Solo in *Star Wars* I was getting a bad feeling about this.

For about 30 minutes, all was good. Over the talkback they said, 'Ah you've got to shift early at this point, you can't rev too high there.'

They could tell that the temperatures were rising.

'Okay,' I said, 'I'm taking it as easy as I can,' and I went down the back straight, through the kink that had been almost impossible in the dark, went through there at 220mph, when suddenly there came an unpleasant sound from the engine. The kind of sound you really don't want to hear from an engine. A shrieking sound of a machine in so much agony that you almost feel sorry for it.

At the same time the rear was moving in an unexpected way, and the sound from the engine began to rise. It was the sound of the engine eating itself, and at almost exactly the same time as I resigned myself to thinking, Game over, it blew up and I pulled off to the inside of the track, the car a non-runner.

And that was it. We had half an hour to go. Just 30 minutes and we would have completed Le Mans, and although we would have been in last place that was infinitely preferable to being a DNF.

It was painful. I've got to admit that I got pretty emotional about it all. I clambered out of the car feeling absolutely despondent, dragging my helmet off my head and plonking myself against a barrier. Not far away a huddle of fans were being really supportive, 'Oh, so sorry, JB,' and stuff that I was really grateful to hear (I hope that I showed it, but apologies if I didn't).

As ever in a situation like that it was the team I felt most sorry for. The mechanics had been up for 48 hours. Me, I'd been sleeping and resting and messing about catching balls while they've been flat out working, so I really felt for them. This was their first year in Le Mans as a team and the aim was just to get to the end and neither us nor our sister car was able to achieve that.

For me, I just wanted to see that chequered flag. I wanted to see that look on the faces of the team when we came in having completed this marathon race. I was sad for the other drivers but I was more sad for everyone else. That feeling of deflation was a communal thing.

I stood out there a while, watching all the cars coming past, which was quite weird. The Toyotas were cruising past, nose to tail, which was a bit sad to see. As for the rest of the field, you could tell that fatigue had set in. Drivers were taking it easy, lifting off early, saving the brakes, a very different proposition to the beginning of the race when it was all guns blazing and loads of overtaking action.

Next I clambered on the back of a steward's motorbike for the trip back to the paddock and a round of commiserations with the team.

What struck me on arrival was that most of our team were French, and so to get a win on French soil would have meant a great deal to them. What I'd loved about them during our short time together was their sheer passion for the racing. A total breed unto themselves, they loved a smoke. Bear in mind this was in 2018, not 1978. I'd never seen so much smoking. Same with the coffee. There was always a queue for the espresso machine a mile long. I mean, I like a coffee, but these guys...

However, there is a happy ending to all of this, because the World Endurance Championships, which is the Championship you need to enter in order to compete at Le Mans, took us next to Silverstone where we were running in third when we had an engine failure. Then Fugi, where we had a starter motor issue, which was a shame because our pace was good and we actually led about ten laps in a wet-dry race. And then on to Shanghai – the six hours of Shanghai race.

In practice, we were quite competitive. In fact, in wet practice, I was quickest in one of the sessions – quicker than the Toyotas after which I could have left happy, right there and then.

Qualifying came round, and it was dry. However, we had a suspension problem, which meant we had massive bouncing while under load in corners. You'd come through the corners, get to the apex and the car would start jumping across the circuit.

As a result we qualified sixth, so not very good at all, but at least they fixed the problem for the race. Meanwhile, the race started and the rain was torrential. I mean, *torrential*. Very much like that race in Brazil, in fact, only without the accompanying loss of nerve, thankfully.

So, we started. I was running third behind the Toyotas and then the race was red-flagged because it was too wet, so I sat in the car for ages, got out, had a pee, got back in and they said, 'Right, the race is going to start,' and off we went behind the safety car.

A couple of cars spun off, even though we were going really slowly. So they red-flagged it again. Restarted it, the pace was good and by the time I brought it in for the changeover, we were third.

Mikhail got in. It was still pissing down with rain. He did a good job, kept it in third, and then it was Vitaly's turn. He jumped in and it was all going okay until he lost it in one of the corners, spun off and spent almost an entire minute trying to get back on the circuit, during which time he was caught by one of the Rebellions. Not overtaken – not yet – but the Rebellion was on new tyres and was five seconds a lap quicker, so it was just a matter of time.

All looked lost. From a third-place podium finish we were about to drop to fourth with just three laps to go. Plus it was getting dark.

Next, Vitaly had to pit for new tyres. It seemed crazy at the time because if he pitted then we'd surely be overtaken, but wouldn't you know it, the safety car came out, and so Vitaly pitted, was really quick in the pits and came out still ahead of the Rebellion but *on new tyres*.

Now he was four seconds quicker than the Rebellion and in the pits we were gnawing our fists. We were like, 'Just keep calm, you're on new tyres, it's going to be easy, you've just got to stay in front.'

He crossed the finish line in third. It was pissing down with rain, it was dark and it was mega, because it was the team's first podium, which made it a really special race for us. I've never seen a group of French people so happy, jumping up and down and high-fiving, hugging. They even put their cigarettes down.

Off we went to the podium together, and who should be there but Fernando, and – wait for it – it was the first time we'd ever shared a podium together since the 2012 Brazilian Grand Prix. Can you believe that?

I'd like to say the moment was very special for us both, but it wasn't. I don't think it really occurred to us at the time.

FACES AND PLACES

1. THE PEOPLE

At the top of the tree are the big bosses…

There's no logical reason why you can't get on well with a team owner. But for some reason you never really do. Is there a psychiatrist on board who can explain why there's always an element of awkwardness at play? I'm telling you, a shrink would have a field day listening in on some of the awkward, stilted conversations that take place between a driver and a team owner. Even Martin Whitmarsh at McLaren, with whom I got on really well, always maintained a certain distance. And as for Ron Dennis…

Why? I just can't say. And I even wonder if it's something that I'm inventing, but then again, no, and I'm sure it was on both sides. Perhaps it's the sums of money involved. The danger. Maybe it's because they've employed you as the star driver and they don't want to get too close; they want to maintain that employer–employee relationship, knowing that one day they might have to give you your marching orders.

Luckily, of course, we drivers can keep the awkward team-owner-encounter dynamic to a minimum, and when it comes to financial matters we have managers to sort our shit out (not literally), and that can be all kinds of hilarious because team owners tend to dislike managers. They dislike them because they don't trust them.

They have good reason, because it's true that lot of managers are not straightforward with team owners, but then they're probably the managers who aren't straight with the driver, either. They're the managers you can't trust. And believe you me, there are a lot of untrustworthy managers out there,

Me, I had to kiss a lot of frogs before I found my… well, let's not get carried away, but Richard's a diamond. Team owners don't like working with him because they know he's hardnosed, but they also know he's better than the alternative because he's honest. He doesn't bullshit, he says it how it is, and I think they respect that he plays hardball. 'You put this in the contract or he won't drive.' But he's also a lovely character, and he can have a joke with the team owners.

As for me and him, there's a lot of trust and respect. We don't always see eye to eye, and we argue, but in the end I know he's got my best interests at heart, which is the most important thing. He was introduced to me by my dad, which says it all, really.

Anyway, back to team owners, and in reverse chronological order…

Ron Dennis

My boss at McLaren was a contradictory guy. Still is, no doubt. Ron loves to talk, but he's also quite shy. He has a famous, almost obsessive, love of the colour grey, but he's actually quite a colourful, emotional character. Loves being the centre of attention. Appears awkward and ill at ease when the spotlight is on him. You see what I mean?

One thing that never changes, though, is that he's a very clever guy, and a very shrewd businessman.

I don't know anyone else like him, but I do have a lot of respect for him, even though we didn't always get on, especially when I tried to get out of my contract at one point. Not to go into too many details, but he was like, 'No, you can't get out of the contract.'

I said, 'Ron, you don't want a driver driving for you who doesn't want to drive.'

Ah, but we reached a compromise in the end, and when I decided to leave, he was cool with it. He used me a lot for sponsor events and, as I said, I enjoyed it. It was good fun and I liked working with him.

Martin Whitmarsh, of course, was team principal, and I got on really well with him. We'd go out for meals, and I think he appreciated the fact that my arrival at the team had lightened the atmosphere a bit. I liked him a lot, actually. He was one of the few people who would stand up to Ron. Never minced his words.

Ross Brawn

Ross was great. A real talismanic presence. He would never lose his cool, never scream or shout. I remember when Brawn scored its first one–two on what was our very first Grand Prix, seeing him going absolutely nuts. It was a joy to witness because he was normally such a calm and controlled presence.

What's more, the car he'd built was absolutely brilliant. You may or may not be familiar with the term 'architect's window'. An architect will include a window on his drawings knowing that it will draw the client's attention and be vetoed. This way the architect gets his other ideas approved 'under the radar', as it were, because all the attention is on the window.

Brawn's 'double diffuser' was a bit like that. All the attention of the other teams, the press, the fans and the FIA was on the diffuser.

'Everybody's looking at the double diffuser and they're not paying attention to what else is on the car,' Ross told me one day. 'Plenty of little tricks on it.'

Things didn't end as well as they could have done between me and Ross. He thought I was making a mistake going off to McLaren and told me so, but I was feeling the McLaren call for a variety of reasons and that was that. He was fairly cool about it, though. (The chief executive Nick Fry was not so cool but that's another story, and one that's already been told.)

Flavio Briatore

He was the Benetton team boss who was my overlord in my second and third season in F1, who called me a lazy playboy.

Later on, when I was at Brawn he called me a *paracarro*, which translates as concrete bollard or something similar.

So, a bit of a turkey, in other words. Flavio based his whole persona on being a flamboyant Italian. And with that came a very outspoken side. Except that he tended to reserve his most flamboyant and outspoken moments for when the cameras and tape recorders were running. In private, to your face, he was actually really nice, when you could understand a word he was saying. But then he'd go off and say something to the press that contradicted what he'd just said to you in private and you found yourself wondering, *Well, which is it, mate? Is it this way, that you've just told me in the office, or is it the other way, that you've just told the press in the paddock?*

Like I say, I prefer people who are straightforward. Whether they like me or not, or we get on, I don't care, it's understanding a character and someone that's honest that matters most to me, especially when you're working with them, like…

Frank Williams

Frank couldn't have been more different from Flavio, being very straight-talking, very up front. As a result, I got on really well with him. There were 'issues' in that particular relationship, of course, because although Frank had taken me on at Williams as a rookie in 2000, he also had Juan Pablo Montoya waiting in the wings. At the same time I was having some personal problems, making the headlines for the wrong reasons, etc. And then Frank announced that Juan Pablo Montoya was going to take my seat.

So that wasn't great, and it sent me off to Benetton where for a while I had a torrid time under Flavio. But I didn't and still don't hold it against Frank. We've shaken hands over it. Let's face it, nobody's going to hold a grudge against Frank. He's one of the true giants of the sport.

And then you have your rivals...

Depending on your reading speed you are, in about a minute, going to hear me go on about how your teammate is your biggest rival.

However, at the risk of dismantling everything I'm about to say on that, you still have to have a rival from another team. Step forward, Mr Sebastian Vettel.

We've always had a good personal relationship – he recently asked me to swap crash helmets, in fact – and on the podium at Abu Dhabi in 2010 when he'd won the Championship and thus taken it off me, he said, 'I'm really happy to be standing up here with you, it really means a lot,' which was a very cool moment, because the previous year we'd been on that same podium and I was World Champion and he was the guy who had been fighting me for it. So, yes, we've always had a good relationship.

Having said all that, the competition has frequently been fierce, and we've certainly had our moments together. There was

Spa in 2010, and, of course, there was the incident in Suzuka, the thrills and spills of which I've covered already. After which there was a bit of bad feeling.

Me and him never shouted at one another, though. We have more respect for each other than all that. Plus we both know that the minute you start shouting you've lost the argument. Like if you start yelling at a bloke, the chances are that he's going to start yelling back and any point you were hoping to make will be lost in the ensuing chaos, as cups of tea are upturned and vases of flowers sent flying. But go to him and make your point calmly and diplomatically, even if the point you're making boils down to 'You're an idiot,' and he's more likely to reflect and maybe even repent.

Needless to say, I follow Seb's career with interest. He's a four-time World Champion, he's obviously very talented, but I don't think his current car is the right fit for him. Not only is the car not quick enough, but he's also making mistakes and it's surprising to see how many he's made this year. He's spun off quite a few times, hit the wall in testing as well in Monaco, had a couple of tangles, including a nasty little incident with Max at Silverstone. He'll be back, though.

Unless he retires, in which case he probably won't be.

But really, it's all about the teammates

I cannot say this often enough, but you have to beat your teammate. It really is the only true competition in the sport. You might not be winning a race – well, you definitely won't be unless you're driving for one of the big three – or you might be winning, or you might have technical problems or you might not.

Doesn't matter. You have to beat your teammate.

After a race, you'll get changed, shower, and then go into your meeting at which all the engineers and strategists will usually be present. After that, you go into a private talk with your race engineer and your data engineer. Usually, you'll have kept something back from the other meeting that you'll share with your engineers. A little secret titbit for their eyes and ears only.

At the same time you'll all be super aware that he'll be doing the same thing. You'll also be aware that the walls have ears. It makes for a really strange, surreal environment. You're kind of at war, but pretending not to be. It's the reason why if something's bothering you, you tend not to make too much of a fuss about it because you don't want it spilling over into bad feeling. It's like a marriage that both parties are desperately trying to keep off the rocks.

In Turkey in 2010, the two Red Bulls in front of Lewis and me in our McLarens wiped each other out. (And there is nothing more embarrassing than wiping out your teammate, etc. etc.) I closed in on Lewis and readied for an overtake.

Meanwhile, he was on the radio, having been asked to conserve fuel, saying, 'Is Jenson going to overtake me?'

'No,' he was told, 'he won't.'

But I never got that memo, and I passed him.

Next came some exciting racing that ended up with him first, me second (the official gap between us was 0.0 seconds), after which he said, 'Did you pass me against team orders?'

'No,' I said, somewhat puzzled at how irate he seemed, given that he had in fact won the race.

After that he decided that the team were taking my side against him, which actually, when you think about it, makes no logical sense, because in a one–two situation almost nobody in the team gives a toss about who's first and who's second.

It was just a miscommunication, but we drivers tend to get very emotional, especially if we think that the team are backing your teammate more than you.

For example, Daniel Ricciardo, who was with Red Bull for years, had Max Verstappen as a teammate. Max came in, super young, super fast, won races. He didn't really outperform Daniel, but they were on a par. However, Daniel felt they were backing Max more – apparently, Max was on more money than him – so he left and went to Renault and now he's got a long-term contract with them.

I don't see Renault winning a race in the next three or four years, whereas at Red Bull he'd be fighting for a podium the whole time and there's always the possibility of winning a race. But he's moved, maybe because he's got too emotionally attached to the idea that he needs to have equal treatment and maybe doesn't feel he was getting it at Red Bull.

By rights, we should all just think, 'You know what? I can do my talking on the track,' but that's easier said than done and it's all too common to get hung up on perceptions of the way you feel you're being treated.

When it comes to the essential difference between you and your teammate, the equipment is, of course, the same, but you can adjust your car to work differently from his and sometimes you do go in a totally different direction, one that suits you more, and your teammate might be fine with that.

Ditto the reverse situation. As far as I'm concerned, he can do what he wants, I feel that I've done the best set-up I can for me.

But then if your teammate's quicker and he's done a different set-up, you'll be like, 'Hang on, I want to try and work out why he's quicker. Can we do his set-up?' And you might copy it. You might choose his base set-up and then make your own little refinements, hoping that you can improve on his. Maybe he likes more understeer, or you like the car a bit low at the rear to give you more traction.

There's no harm in a bit of in-house fighting, of course, especially if there's no other team in serious contention. That was why the in-house fighting between Nico Rosberg and Lewis was great, because no one else could touch them. Mercedes were so much faster that you *had* to have in-house fighting, or else it was a boring weekend.

Same at McLaren when it was Alain Prost and Ayrton Senna. They were a second and a half quicker than anyone else. People forget that. It was the best racing of F1 history, they say. No, it wasn't. Those guys could be almost a lap down and still win the race, so it was all about beating their teammate, and that's why there was so much passion and, I guess, a bit of hatred between them, because all they had to do was beat each other.

As they both knew, it hurts when a teammate kicks your arse. I had that with Checo Pérez in 2013. Lewis had just left and because he was so shit-hot I assumed that nobody could come in and be close to him.

Then at the third race, in Bahrain, Checo aggressively overtook me, pushing me out wide in the process.

I got on the radio, bit cross about that, feeling like he was taking the piss. Then I overtook him, and then he tried to overtake me back and we made contact and I was back on the radio complaining about it, after which he beat me in the race.

Not a great day for me. And afterwards, I was pretty pissed off about it and made my feelings known. I was so angry the way he was driving, and even said so in the press (in the diplomatic, euphemistic way we do in Formula One: 'Soon something serious will happen so he has to calm down. He's extremely quick and he did a great job today but some of it is unnecessary and an issue when you are doing those speeds.').

It took me a few races to work out that I wasn't really angry at him for the way he was driving, because he was racing and, after all, that's what we're paid to do, otherwise it's not sport, it's a catwalk for cars. I was just angry because he'd beaten me, simple as that.

For his part, he was hungry for the win and didn't care that I was his teammate. Fair play to him, he went out and proved himself, and in retrospect, I was jealous and upset that he'd come out on top. See? Told you we had thin skins. And once I came to that conclusion we became great teammates and he was the guy who surprised me most out of all my teammates, which I suppose is something else you need to factor into the strange teammates' brew: that need to impress your teammate, earn his respect – and he certainly did that.

Checo left for Force India and was replaced by Kevin Magnussen for a year, before Fernando Alonso joined in 2015 – a return for him, in fact, since he'd previously partnered Lewis at McLaren.

It's fair to say that Fernando turning up at McLaren came as a bit of surprise to many of us. He had left Ferrari because he wasn't happy there and he felt that he should have been winning titles, but even so, he left a team that was winning in order to join a team that was middle of the pack, or even near the back of the pack.

Why? Well, for him, probably the money. But for the team which has to find that money in order to employ a top driver that probably won't bring them any extra silverware?

Well, at first blush, it's a situation that provides an instant, short-term boost right across the board. The team wants the best driver line-up because it gives a lift to the mechanics and the engineers, it elevates the team in the eyes of the watching world. Everyone was like, 'Wow, McLaren have got two World Champions and one of them's Fernando Alonso, one of the biggest talents the sport's ever seen.'

So that's good. For a while.

But of course what ultimately happens is that the results don't come rolling in, and it serves as a painful reminder that simply having a great driver line-up isn't enough in Formula One, because drivers are only one part of the formula. Next, the team will get to wondering whether all that money being used to pay the drivers couldn't be going on developing the car. And maybe, who knows? They might have a point about that. The whole thing is such a high-wire balancing act.

For the driver, you have to wonder if a move like that is worth it. Sure, Fernando had a lot of money in the bank, but he also had to watch other people win World Championships that conceivably could have been his. At the kind of level we're talking about, that means more than money. Plus, I doubt Fernando was getting paid poorly at Ferrari.

Still, I liked having him as a teammate. Lewis was quick but as I've already said, Fernando was a much more 'complete' driver. In him I had probably the toughest teammate in the world and as a result you raise your game (not like you're slacking before, but you know what I mean), and when I finished in front of him at the weekend, it was a proper buzz. It was like winning a race.

He hated it when that happened. I'm not saying he was a poor loser, but... well, in my opinion, he was a bit of a poor loser

All of which is not to say that we weren't friendly. We were. Just that we both wanted to finish above the other. We knew we weren't going to win any races or step on the podium, so beating each other was all the competition we had. Beating each other in qualifying, beating each other in the race.

Fernando could be quite publicly critical of the car, and he got a bit of flak for that. Deservedly so, in my opinion. I'd say if the car was tough to drive, but I wouldn't criticise it, or the team, because that would hurt the team and it would hurt the sponsors. Everyone knows that the car's not good enough. We all know that Fernando Alonso's not driving slowly, but sharing your frustrations publicly doesn't help anyone.

For me, it worked in my favour. The team would be more supportive of me, because I wasn't putting them down. It wasn't like I was blowing smoke up their arses. I'd tell them that things were wrong. I'm not one of these drivers who go, 'It's all right, it's going to be fine.' I tell them the issues, just as much as Fernando did. But I did it in a different manner, behind closed doors. Which is the way it should be.

I think the teammate I've had the best relationship with was Rubens Barrichello, who was my teammate at Brawn. I'm not saying that we always saw eye to eye – we didn't, because we were teammates, and like I say, it's always the elephant in the room – but we got on. Rubens is a lovely bloke. Like a lot of Brazilians, he's a real family man, but when he's in the factory or at the circuit, he's 100 per cent focused on the job at hand. He understands the car better than anyone, better than me, even, which was definitely a strength of his and meant that having him as a teammate really helped me develop as a driver.

A bunch of us have appeared on *Top Gear* over the years. Michael did it, Kimi did it, Lewis, myself, and Rubens.

Of us all, Rubens was the only one to beat the Stig so he got us all T-shirts made. His said, 'I beat the Stig', and ours all said, 'I got beaten by the Stig'.

Not everyone wore theirs. I did though.

And then there's Lewis. He may not have been as good as I was at doing voiceovers for *Tooned*, but he was certainly the fastest driver I ever had as a teammate.

Not only that, but he's the real big character of the sport. He's got 11 million followers on Instagram, He's huge on Twitter. He's one of the few current Formula One drivers who is a household name.

I think he's probably one of these guys who's done an awful lot of growing up in the public eye. I mean, he came into the sport as a phenomenal talent, and that has never dimmed, obviously, but in terms of his skill at presentation, it's come on leaps and bounds. I remember getting ready for events with him and he'd look at me, wanting tips on how to look, and now he's a fashion guru.

I always remember him trying to think of something to say. If I said something in an interview and it was his turn, he'd look at me and go, 'I was going to say that, I don't know what to say now. I don't know how to better that.'

I'd be like, 'Mate, it's not about bettering me. It's not laps on the circuit. We're just saying how we feel about a situation, about how that race went,' But he never really got that. He always felt that he should go one better.

Like I say, though, he's developed an awful lot. The Lewis Hamilton I know is a great person, but I think that a lot of people in F1 don't get him because he leads a very different lifestyle, and I think he's looked upon as being quite American in his outlook. What his detractors forget, though, is that he's got a lot of people interested in the sport who weren't interested before, and a lot of those will be Americans. What's more, the chances are he's going to go on and dominate the sport for years to come, and he will, of course, deserve every success that comes to him, because you don't get it unless you're very talented, which he is, and prepared to learn and work hard, which he is.

Who can stop him, though? That's the question. And the answer it seems is Max Verstappen. This is a guy who's come in, been bloody quick and won his first race in Barcelona, which was either the best thing that could have happened to him or the worst, because on the one hand his confidence bloomed and on the other hand he thought he was invincible, at which point the crashes started coming, the mistakes, the incidences of him losing his head. You don't need to push as hard in practice as he was. He crashed in Monaco last year before qualifying started, destroyed the car and didn't qualify as a result.

It's a well-worn scenario. It's happening to Charles Leclerc right now – another very raw talent still being fine-tuned. A version of it happens to a lot of drivers, yours truly included. The true test of racing character is whether the driver can come out the other side, and while it's taken Max a while to learn from his mistakes, and work out that you need to ease off every now and then, I think he's really getting there now.

To me, it feels like he's much more like the finished article now. Not *the* finished article. But getting there. His natural ability is being better managed. He's much more balanced and as a result he's been finding a lot more consistency, and for me he's probably been the driver of the year in 2019.

2. THE PLACES

The problem with designing new circuits is that they cost a fortune, so there aren't many new ones, which is why city-centre circuits, like the new Hanoi Street Circuit debuting in 2020, are where it's at.

And that's good, because street circuits are kind of fun. But at the same time you don't want too many of them, because they're very difficult to overtake on. You don't have the run-offs and braking zones that you get on the custom-built circuits, whereas on a lot of the street circuits there's no run-off. There are just walls. And if you have a brake failure you're going to meet one of those in a big hurry.

Saying that, there's an upside. Having no run-offs reduces the temptation to overdrive the car, unlike somewhere like Austin or Malaysia where all that space tempts you into taking risks that may ultimately derail you. Instead, you build up to getting the maximum out of the car, you work up to finding your limit, rather than going over and pulling back, which to me is the essence of good racing.

From a driving point of view, though, the circuits I like are the fast, flowing ones like Suzuka and Spa, which have a mix of tricky corners and ones that you can take almost flat-out.

It's the same with Le Mans. There are two corners that I really don't like at Le Mans, and they didn't suit the car we were driving. You'd brake and the car wouldn't slow down enough, and you'd turn in and you get understeer and only just about make it round. Ah, but every other corner on the circuit was just awesome, just lovely and flowy and smooth, and it's such an amazing experience driving at night.

However, I have a rule in Formula One when it comes to the best circuits for visiting. Not necessarily driving, but visiting. And it's the three Ms: **Montreal, Melbourne** and **Monaco**.

Montreal is a street circuit, and basically the city stops, just like a city-wide festival. There are a couple of places where all the restaurants get marquees out into the street, and it's party time, day and night. It's a very special atmosphere.

As a driver, if you're staying in the city, it's a nightmare, because you can't get around, so you leave the circuit and there's no way to reach your hotel. Sometimes you've got to walk, which is unusual, but for most of us is a really welcome change of pace. I've mentioned before how being in Formula One is like being in a never-changing city: Formulaoneville. Well, Montreal is where you do actually get to see a bit of your host city for that reason, and very beautiful it is too.

My first ever race in Montreal was 2000. Me and my dad and various others went to a party hosted by the owner of Cirque du Soleil at his huge house, and it was there that we found ourselves sitting around a bonfire singing 'Yellow Submarine' with none other than George Harrison. Pretty surreal. Trouble was, I was really tired, so I said to Dad who, bear in mind, was sitting around a bonfire singing Beatles songs with George Harrison, 'Dad, I'm going to have to go. You stay. Enjoy yourself.'

He was like, 'Uh uh, no. We go together.' But anyway, as it happened, the quiet Beatle – who it turned out wasn't all that quiet – was ready to leave, and so he jumped in our limo with us. Off we went home with George sticking his head out of the limo sunroof, still singing Beatles songs. That was an incredible, very special experience – one that opened both our eyes to this wonderful world we were suddenly a part of.

Melbourne, meanwhile, is a bit hit and miss with parties but it's a fun race to go to, because there's a good atmosphere and it's the first Grand Prix of the year, and everyone's really excited to see what the new cars look like and how they perform. It's in a park, of course. Albert Park, which is beautiful.

And then there's **Monaco**, which encapsulates all the glamour of Formula One. It's the oldest race. It's yachts and film stars and models, and lots of racing drivers live there.

These are the little things that all add up to Monaco's very, very special atmosphere.

Meanwhile, for a driver it's great, too. You never feel more alive than when you're wrestling this 900 horsepower monster around its streets. Coming out at the end of a lap around Monaco, especially when you've done a good lap and you've pushed the car to the limit, there's nothing like it. It's scary but also immensely rewarding. There's no other place that you qualify and enjoy it as much as Monaco. It's physically and mentally another level compared to anywhere else.

Then, at night-time, all hell breaks loose, because you get parties on boats, parties in nightclubs like Amber Lounge, or in bars like La Rascasse, which is a bar on the second-to-last corner. When the circuit opens back up to the public at night, La Rascasse spills out into the street, so, at midnight, 1am, you've got drunk people drinking on the street, on the race circuit, spilling their beer on the track. It's complete madness. There are scooters parked everywhere and then parties finish at I-don't-know-when in time for the big clear-up before testing begins at 9am.

About seven in the morning, all the scooters that have been left by revellers are taken to the police station. I mention the scooters in particular because I once lent my PR guy, James, my scooter. He left it on the street outside La Rascasse and then staggered back to a boat. The next morning, he awoke, groggy, groaning and massaging his sore head. Where am I? Oh, that's right, I'm on a boat in Monaco harbour having gone out and got absolutely trashed last night. Where's Jenson's scooter? Oh, that's right, I left it on the road outside the bar. What's that sound?

Oh my God, it's racing cars.

James leapt out of bed running to the prow of the boat, only to run straight into a glass door, knocking himself out. By the time he came round he had a lump on his head the size of an egg and a monumental task ahead: to recover my scooter on race day in Monaco.

Credit, though. He found it. Took him the whole of race day, and he had to pay the Monaco fuzz a massive fine, but he got the scooter back.

Salutary tale there.

Okay, one more M. It's **Monza**, which because you've got Milan down the road is actually great for parties. Like Monaco, it's one of the big races, and a lot of that is down to the Italian fans, the famous *tifosi*. They pack the place – a beautiful park, it is – every seat in the grandstand is taken. People drive their caravans up to the edge of the circuit so they can stand on top of them to see. People hang off walls, hang off signs to watch the race. It's a really special atmosphere, even for a driver not driving a Ferrari.

In 2011, I was leading for a lot of the race until Fernando, who was driving for Ferrari, jumped on me in the pit stops, and I ended up finishing second. Got up to the podium and the fans were booing me. I was like *Really? You're booing me? A Ferrari has won, for crying out loud.*

But that's Monza for you. And after all, the partisan crowd is an essential part of the whole experience there. If you're on the podium with two Ferrari drivers, it's mega – all you see is a sea of people all the way down the straight, a field of red in the stands. You forget about the cameras, the TV audience, you're just totally in that moment, where the excitement of the crowd is so infectious and intoxicating that it takes you to a whole other level. It really is very special indeed.

If the three Ms are the circuits that are the best to visit for whatever reason, then there are the three Ss which are the best for the racing itself. **Silverstone** is fast, it's flowing, you're rarely below 130mph. It's just crazy how fast it is. I remember going there back in 1994 with my dad. We camped and I recall standing on the banks and watching the cars come through. It's the best race to see an F1 car up close.

Spa is another one. A great driver's circuit. My favourite, though, is **Suzuka**, which is flowing, narrow, old school. You're on the edge the whole time, knowing that if you make a mistake, it's going to end in tears, which is good for the same reasons it's good to race on a road track: you build up to your limit rather than overreach and have to pull back.

I won there in 2011 with McLaren when I finished first, Fernando second and third was Sebastian, who clinched his second World Championship the same day that I won. So, a great race, on a very special circuit. In qualifying, when you're on low fuel and new tyres, you feel like you're a superhero driving this 900-horsepower car from turn two up to turn eight. There's so much downforce you can only just about keep up with where the circuit's going.

Mind you, the problem is that a lot of the circuits I've talked about and the circuits that I love are probably not the best circuits for overtaking. If you've qualified at the front it's great, but if you've qualified tenth then you know you've got a battle on your hands.

Compare it to Austin, a great circuit because you can have some really good battles. There are five places at which you can overtake, which means that if you do happen to find yourself in tenth, you have chance of clawing back the places, and the fight is awesome. If you make your move then the guy will come back at you at the next corner and vice versa. You can overtake down the inside on the back straight and he'll go round the outside at the next one and then you'll be on the inside for the next corner. It's just brilliant. Added to that, Austin has a very unusual night-life situation in that it's kind of dead during the day but once the sun goes down it's like a different place. There's one particular road through the city that comes alive.

And lastly, and although I hate to end on a downbeat note, an A.

Abu Dhabi, my least favourite circuit, was never exactly fun, it was very stop-start. There were no real fun fast sections. It was like straight, brake hard, 90-degree corner, straight, brake, left, 90-degree corner. Very angular circuit.

Still, that's like saying what's your least favourite Ben & Jerry's flavour. I mean, they're all pretty good.

THE
PERFECT
LAP

Is there such a thing as the perfect lap? I don't know. How about the nicest teammate who lets you share all his data, and a team with loads of money who want to give tons of it to you. No sponsor days. A car with an inbuilt seat massage and great visibility, no buffeting or vibrations. And when you cross the finish line, it says to you, 'Well done, JB, you're on pole position', because, of course, you're always on pole position.

No?

All right, then. How about…

THE OCCASION

Qualifying. Sorry race-day fans, but it's qualifying. The reason why is because you've built up to it. You've gone through testing, you've gone through practice and, in theory, at least – this being the perfect lap, after all – you've fine-tuned and perfected the car to within an inch of its life. So you might have had too much understeer in practice, and that was a pain, because if you're anything like me, you hate understeer. But you've adjusted that. It might have been bouncing too much in the high-speed corner. But you've tweaked the suspension to deal with that. You might have had second thoughts about the tyres you're using, but you're happy now.

In short, you've achieved all you can with the car to make it as quick as possible. You have confidence in yourself and in the car and now, for the qualifying session, you're going to give the engine full power, because you never do for testing or practice, you always leave a little juice in reserve, never maximum power, only for qualifying and the race. For the first time all weekend you're really going to let the tiger out of the cage.

Lastly, as this is the 'perfect' lap, and I get to choose exactly *when* I get to drive it would be first thing in the morning. Nothing to do with the temperature or the height of the sun or anything like that – just because I want to get on with it. Nothing grinds my gears more than race day when you wake up at 8am and it feels like hours before you even get to the warm-up lap.

THE CAR

I need a car that has a really good strong rear stability in order to banish that pesky oversteer. That's the ideal – a car that gives good front grip so the more you turn the wheel, the more front grip you get – the kind of grip that pulls you around the corner as though the car is on rails.

It's a balanced car, that's what it's all about. When I brake, I brake hard and then come off. But I'm modulating a little bit, balancing the car as I come off the brake pedal, and when I go on the throttle, I'm modulating again, so I'm playing with the steering, I'm trying to be as smooth as I can with the steering wheel. But when I'm throttling, I'm gradually finding the grip, so I get on the power, feel just a little bit of wheel spin, hold it there until the wheel spin stops and then I'll come on with more power, more power, more power.

All my movements are through my pedals, if you like. So I brake and then I modulate that and then throttle, I'm modulating all the way through the corner.

Lewis, on the other hand, is the opposite. Lewis arrives at a corner, bang on the brake, and whether he's braked in the right place or not, he just immediately comes off the brake, no modulation and the throttle, gets to the apex and he gets to an exit, and he's like – *bang* – there's nothing, it's like his legs are just, like *bang, bang, bang*, and it shouldn't work – it's a style of driving that's completely opposite to mine but it works because he does everything through the steering wheel, so instead of modulating these pedals, which is what I'd do, he's modulating the steering; he's accelerating and controlling the car through his hands rather than his feet.

Honestly. It's amazing. You open our data, it's, like, oh my God, it's crazy how we're so different and yet we would do pretty much the same lap time.

WEATHER

It's dry and the temperature is low. With low circuit temperatures, you get more grip, the engine runs better. So an ambient temperature of 15 degrees would be ideal, I guess. The circuit would end up being 22 degrees, probably.

In winter testing you always go really quick because the circuit's cold. Then you'd go back to the same circuit when it's hot, it's often windier too, and you go slower. And yes, while we're on the subject: wind can make a lot of difference with aerodynamics. Say if you've got a headwind in a corner, you're going to get a lot more front grip, whereas if you have the wind behind you, you'll get understeer through that corner.

At Suzuka, because of the way the circuit's designed, you get a tail wind on the straights, so you go quicker on the straights, so you're gaining time there, and then you turn, and you've got all these S-bends and you have a head wind all the way up the S-bends, which is amazing, because you get so much downforce on the car.

It's like it's on rails the whole way around Suzuka. It's one of the reasons I love it so much. You gain a second a lap time if you have the wind in that direction, whereas if it's blowing the other way you get a headwind on the straight, so the car goes slower and you get a tail wind, up through the S's, and you've got no grip.

Suzuka is the extreme but that happens on a lot of circuits. If the wind changes it's tough and you can also get gusty weather as well. I've had times on a qualifying lap where suddenly I've lost all my grip and they look at the data and they say, 'Yeah, it's a gust of wind, you just got unlucky.'

I'm like, 'You're kidding me, no one's going to believe that it was a gust of wind.' And lots of drivers say it and you think, *Is it true or not?* but normally it is. You can get real unlucky with a nasty gust of wind.

CIRCUIT

Friday is when you first start driving and normally the circuit at this point is very dusty. 'Green', they call it, which means it's not at its best and won't be until you get to qualifying.

It's another reason that qualifying is the best time to drive, because by then the circuit is what they call 'rubbered in'. See, all the teams have brand-new tyres so the rubber goes down and cleans the circuit and gives the track grip. This is why it's so great in qualifying. It's hit that sweet spot you want. Whereas for the race it's very different, because in the race, you get a lot of the tyres throwing the marbles off.

It's not a problem if you're on the racing line, but if you stray off that, there's no grip at all. Again, it makes it interesting when you're overtaking. Say if you overtake someone and push them on to the marbles, they can't get you on the exit because they've got dirty tyres.

ACING THOSE CORNERS

And of course the first corner is great. Because like I said, that's the one where you get a feel for the car, for the race and for the task at hand – the one that gives you that confidence going into the rest of the lap.

The only one that's really tricky to do is Monaco, because the first corner has a brick wall in front of you. Well, a metal Armco barrier. After that, with Monaco, as with any other circuit, it's a case of pushing the car to the limit, constantly adjusting the drive to take other elements into consideration.

For example, you know how the car feels, but you don't know what the wind's doing; you don't know if the circuit is as clean as it was the last lap around or as clean as it was that morning.

Every corner is different, so you're always thinking on your feet. You know that if you brake too late then it's game over, but at the same time you're braking as late as you dare and then dealing with whatever happens next, a slight lock-up front or rear; you're adjusting the brake pedal to stop the lock-up because if you've locked up, you will just career straight on, but if you can stop the lock-up, you can get around the corner and not actually lose any time.

On the way out, the quicker you get to full throttle, the quicker you can exit the corner and carry that all the way down the straight. Slightly too early, though, and you've lost the rear end. It'll snap and you get that oversteer and even though it won't spin, you might just be controlling oversteer all the way out and you're not getting that drive out of the corner. So it's a tricky balance between not exiting quick enough and exiting too quickly, which can cause loss of traction and lap time as well.

YOU GET LOADS OF PRACTICE

Knowing the circuit well is, of course, essential, and that comes with experience rather than simulator time, which is only helpful to a degree. In a simulator you can tell which direction you're going in, but you don't get the same sensation, you don't get the feel of the asphalt, you don't get the buffeting.

So it's the practice on the circuit itself which is most important. And you do get a lot of practice: two one-and-a-half-hour sessions on Friday and then an hour session on Saturday before qualifying. If you want to, you can do a lot of laps.

The idea is that you do runs with low fuel, with high fuel, on new tyres, old tyres, to get a real feel for the race and for the circuit. Now if, for some reason, you've had an issue that means you miss half of your practice, it always makes it a bit trickier, there's a lot more pressure. So practice, practice, practice.

THERE'S NO TRAFFIC

Not just in the race but in qualifying, too. Say you get a car that's done his lap time already and is still driving round. They think they're getting out of the way and not causing you any lap-time loss, but sometimes they are. So if they're 200 metres in front of you in a high-speed corner, they're still hurting the airflow on to your car, which changes your balance a little bit. They'll say they're not affecting you, and people watching it won't think that they're making any difference, because it looks like they're miles in front. But take it from your old pal Jenson it *does* make a difference because of that all-important airflow.

So it's always better when a car sees you coming, pulls over and doesn't get in your way. It's when they go through a few corners with you behind thinking, *Oh he's far enough behind*, that's when it hurts you. Not just because of the aero, actually, but it's also a mental thing. If there's a car in front, it's frustrating. It disrupts your focus at the very moment you want absolute concentration.

NO DISTRACTIONS

There are none anyway, to be honest. You get in the car, you close your visor and you forget about everything else – and that's just natural because you're doing something that you love and something that you feel you're the best at.

The only thing that does cause an issue is if you've had a bad practice. For example, if you've crashed or missed most of practice because you've had an engine failure or an issue with the car. Then you're going into qualifying, thinking, *Shit, I don't really understand where the braking points are. I'm not sure what tyres I should be using.*

Some of the issue is the circuits getting grippier throughout the weekend, and if you missed Saturday morning practice you might not know if you should use the same gear as you did in practice in a certain corner, or a higher gear if the circuit has gripped up. The best thing to do is just relax: you've been in this situation before and you'll adapt very quickly, but it's difficult to tell yourself that in the heat of the moment, when the seconds are counting down to your first lap in qualifying. It feels like turning up to deliver a speech without having rehearsed it enough. You can do it. You know you can do it. Just that you wish you were word perfect. You've got that nagging feeling that you should have done more.

As a result, you have to take a step back a little. You're more cautious, which means you brake a little bit earlier and you're less aggressive with the car, because you're not sure what it's going to do.

Otherwise, though, all things being equal, and assuming you've had a decent practice session, by the time you get to qualifying, you're confident, you know you can do a good job, and no, you don't think about anything else, and I never have. I have never got into a racing car thinking about the outside world. I mean, the team and the people I have around me wouldn't allow it anyway. Everything is done for the express purpose of aiding my focus. My manager Richard would never talk business. If my mum was there, she'd never talk about family stuff. It would just be 'good luck', and I'd get in the car.

There are no media commitments. Oh, there might be a picture with the king of Spain or something like that. But you wouldn't even think about it; it's just part of the day, like having dinner or a massage; it doesn't really mean anything to you. You just get straight into the car and that's what *does* mean everything to you. Recently there was a thing where they took away the grid girls. It was like, what grid girls? You get out to the car on the grid, you talk to your engineer, your physio gives you all your kit to cool down, you drink, you go to the toilet, you rest, you return, ten minutes to go, National Anthem, get in the car...

And you don't notice the grid girls. It just doesn't happen. You're fully focused on the job in hand, which is thinking through the start process: what could go wrong? What's going to go right? How can I get the best out of myself and the car I have? World hunger, the plastic in the ocean. You don't think about it.

And it's funny, because doing a triathlon I'd think about everything because I was trying to take my mind off it. But in an F1 car? Fuhgeddaboutit.

I remember one time leading with maybe 15 laps to go and I found my mind wandering a little. I was thinking ahead to crossing the line, imagining the emotions, thinking about the team, even thinking about having to get out of the car and do the interviews.

And then suddenly I was like, *Snap out of it, Jenson, we're not there yet.*

Still, that was an isolated occurrence. And most of the time I was fighting, anyway. It's very unusual to find yourself on your own on the circuit with no one to overtake or no one trying to overtake you, it was always a battle.

And that, after all, is what makes the perfect lap. Whether you're up against the clock or an opponent, your teammate or yourself, it's about pushing it – it's about taking it to the limit.

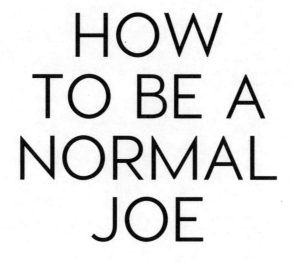

HOW
TO BE A
NORMAL
JOE

1. HOW TO MOVE ON (AND GROW UP)

It wasn't because I wasn't quick any more, because I was. I was still quick, I still had the pace, and I still felt that even though the years of winning races, let alone Championships, were most likely behind me I was still doing a good job.

It was just that the life had taken its toll. The old boy not being there was a big part of it, but on top of that I was just tired. I mean, *proper* tired. Mentally drained. Which drained me physically as well. And what I didn't want to do was let that fatigue affect the job I did. Although tired, I still enjoyed all aspects of life in Formula One, but I didn't want to end up *not* enjoying it, making a half-arsed job of it. I didn't want to end up not giving it 100 per cent.

Thus, I got to the point three years before I retired when I said to my mates and my family that I couldn't do it any more. 'I just want to stop racing.'

I'd had offers to race for other teams – three different ones in all – but nobody was able to offer me a car that could win races, or even be on the podium, so it just wasn't worth it. Yes, there would still have been the competition with my teammate; there would still have been the sponsor work that I enjoy. But that's not enough to compensate for not being competitive, and I definitely wouldn't want to race in F1 if I wasn't winning races. There's little point. The bottom line is that it's stress I don't need for too little reward.

I'm asked now if I'd return if I was offered a drive that would guarantee me wins, and the answer is that I'd probably have a go, yes. If you have the opportunity to win, you take it. I can't see Lewis retiring if he's in a winning car, it just doesn't happen like that. Why would you want to? If you're mentally strong enough and you can take it, and – importantly – you're winning, then you're going to have more highs than lows, and that's going to make it worth doing.

What I'd find more difficult to replace is that raw passion and excitement that a 24-year-old would bring to the game. So while on a good day I'd be great, I know that if I had a bad day I'd let things get to me the way they wouldn't have done 15 or so years previously. I'd be questioning myself. *Why am I doing this? Why am I putting myself through all this?* Whereas a young kid is going to be, like, *Right, that was a tough race, next time I need to do a better job.*

And, to be honest, I know that in racing the bad days are going to outnumber the good days by a ratio of two to one (depending on what you're driving, of course). I look at where I am right now, settled in LA with a fiancée and a baby, and I know that I don't really want those bad days in my life.

Could I have taken time off? I guess so, but I've seen others do it and they've never been quite the same – even Michael Schumacher when he came back was not the same force by any means.

And so I left. *Boom*. Decided to explore my love of racing in other avenues, concentrate on different aspects of my life. And because everything had been done for me in F1, because all I'd had to focus on was driving, fitness and engineering, I suddenly had to become a grown-up. It was like my life had been in a state of suspended animation between the ages of 19 and 37. Big wake-up call.

But I did grow up, and I learnt so much. It was simple things. Putting down roots. Making a home. As I said, I'd never paid a bill in my life and suddenly I was pulling out my hair because they were coming out of nowhere. Before, when somebody else was doing all that for me, I didn't really notice where the money was going, but now my eyes were open to how much I was paying on, say, storage or car insurance, and I could see that there was lot of money being wasted. It's been a bit of an eye-opening experience.

Mainly, though, and at the risk of coming across all Californian for a moment, I've grown as a person. In fact, I think I've improved more as a human being in the last two years than I have in the rest of my life. And that's all down to taking a step back from Formula One, changing my priorities, finding love with Brittny, being a dog-owner, becoming a father…

2. HOW TO COMMENTATE

As well as diving headlong into the world of Super GT, I also landed a job with Sky.

First time was at Silverstone in 2018, and I remember just as I left home on the Wednesday before the race saying to Brit, 'I'm nervous, weirdly.'

She was like, 'That's not weird. You're out of your comfort zone. But you've just got to ask yourself, what's the worst that can happen? What *really* is the worst that can happen?'

I looked at her like she was mad. 'Well, I could make a complete dick of myself in front of millions of people watching.'

'Like?'

'I could stumble over my words.'

She shrugged.

'Get my facts wrong.'

She shrugged.

'Not talk when I'm supposed to talk, and talk when I'm not supposed to.'

She shrugged.

'Look, Jenson, even if you do those things it won't matter, because you're not a broadcaster, you're a racing driver. You're not there to be slick. You're there to bring the knowledge. Now go.'

All so true, of course. Getting someone's name wrong, fumbling your words, making a mistake – so what? This is the white heat of a Grand Prix weekend. You're there to be yourself in front of the cameras.

And so I went along with exactly that philosophy. Just be myself. Except a cool version of myself.

Anyway, what I discovered is that the way it normally works is that you have backup. So I'm the pundit, if you like, and I'm standing there with the regular presenter, usually Simon Lazenby, who in terms of broadcasting does all the heavy lifting.

The weirdest thing is that you hear everything in your earpiece, so, 'Three, two, one...' and then Lazenby will open the show before asking me a question.

The most difficult thing to get your head around is talking and maintaining the thread of whatever it is you're talking about, while in your ear someone is providing you with instructions. So there you are going, 'Blah, blah, Lewis, blah, blah, Sebastian, blah, blah, Max,' while in your ear someone in a distant studio is saying. 'Okay, counting down. Fifteen seconds before you're off-air. And now ten... Nine... Eight...'

That was the worst it got, and certainly that first weekend I was always glad to hand back to Lazenby for whom I developed serious respect, thinking, *I just couldn't do what he's doing, the amount of pressure he's under having to open the show, close it, marshal everything else that's happening in between and do it all with the skill of a seasoned ringmaster.*

And it's funny because when I was a racing driver I'd be opposite these guys thinking they're were doing a simple, straightforward interview. Now I'm on the other side of the fence, I'm suddenly aware of the fact that the interviewer is in fact juggling several balls at once. Who knew?

The next challenge was when they'd get me to interview a driver. Just me and the driver. After qualifying at the Spanish Grand Prix, I went on to the grid and the top-three drivers drove down, all happy, got out of their cars, waving to the crowd, and then it went to a live worldwide feed, just me with the microphone, no one else, somebody would count me down, and it would just be me asking the drivers with no Lazenby to back me up, no one to hand off to if you're lost for words or don't know which direction to go in.

So I'm walking up to Valtteri Bottas who qualified on pole and it was funny because he's waving at the crowd, then he looks at me and he knows who I am and there's a little smile on his face because we've raced together for so many years, and in the past we would have been stood close to one another dealing with interviewers, and now I'm the one asking the stupid questions.

We moved to Lewis and he was a little bit disappointed to be second, but, again, it was cool and there was that connection between us because we're both drivers. After that it was Sebastian, and in fact it was after that interview that he suggested swapping helmets at the next race.

And I got through it. I did it.

What's strange is that when I was a driver I'd chat to other drivers about making that move from driving to TV coverage and we all agreed that we'd never want to. Poacher turning gamekeeper and all that.

But it's weird because once you've been out of the sport for a couple of years, it's actually really good fun. You feel that you can bring something different to the table. You're not just there for window dressing; you can add a dynamic that's otherwise missing, much of which comes from your personal connection to the sport and other drivers. I have so much experience with racing, not just driving the cars, but being in that paddock, which I can bring to the conversations and the interviews.

I spoke to Lewis for a longer interview with him last year at the British Grand Prix. I think it was one of the best interviews we've ever had with him, and it's all down to the fact that we're both drivers and were teammates for three years. He forgets that all the big cameras are there and the world's listening and thinks he's talking to a mate. I could ask him, 'Have you got a girlfriend?' and get away with it. No other journalist could do that.

Of course, if we got to a team boss, it's a bit more of a serious interview. Sky might want me to pose certain questions. But for drivers they normally want me to come up with the questions and ask them from a driver's perspective. I try to steer clear of, 'How did it go?' or, worse, 'How do you feel?' knowing from my years on the other side of the cameras that they are the very worst questions you can be asked, and they tend to be asked by someone who isn't quite sure of their facts, and so is hoping that your answer will give then ammunition to ask more questions.

I mean, really, what can you say to 'how do you feel?'.

'I feel like ripping someone's still-beating heart from their ribcage and eating it whole'?

'Yeah, I feel great, really brilliant' equals 'Oh, he doesn't care / is being sarcastic / is on drugs' etc.

So instead what you get is, 'Well, obviously very disappointed, blah, blah, blah, positives, blah, blah, blah, move on, blah, blah, learn from this, blah, blah,' the same cut-and-paste answer that everybody has heard a zillion times before.

It's a difficult transaction. And while the interviewer needs to get their shit together, the driver can't really afford to act like a prize arse. I've seen interviews where the driver's given one-word answers and I've thought, 'Mate, there are millions of people hanging on your every word here. They want to hear your feelings on the matter.'

It may be that he's annoyed at some of the questions being a bit basic. But that comes with the territory and to most of the people watching, 'How do you feel?' is a perfectly legitimate question. They don't know you've already been asked it half a dozen times that day.

Me, I've got annoyed with silly questions in the past ('Do you want to win?') and I've bitten back, much to my later regret. Fact is, we all get stressed, but if you can come back at it with a better angle, you look like a much better person for answering the question correctly and in a grown-up manner.

So I've come to really enjoy the TV work. Simon Lazenby is great and I'm working with a lot of other ex-F1 drivers, too, which makes it a lot of fun. We all go to dinner in the evenings and there's loads of gossip about who might be moving where, who's unhappy here, who went out and had too much to drink, and so on and so forth.

And of course I love being in the paddock. To be there without the stress of the race is a joy. First of all, walking in is weird. When I'm racing in Japan, there's no hospitality, it's all very simple, it's grass-roots racing. Gradually I'd forgotten how luxurious it is in the world of Formula One. You should see Red Bull's motorhome – it's like a cruise liner. Maybe it was always like that. Just that for the first time since entering the sport I'm able to take my time and enjoy these sights. As a driver you're fixated on getting from getting from A to B in the shortest possible time to minimise time spent doing selfies. You hardly even lift your head let alone stop to admire the scenery. But as a newly minted pundit I felt like one of those kids chosen to take a tour of Willy Wonka's Chocolate Factory, looking around, going, 'Ooh' and 'Aah' and noticing things I'd never seen before. I still get someone saying hello or wanting an autograph or a selfie, but it's a lot more relaxed because people aren't there for the likes of me, they're looking out for the drivers. Being in this position has revitalised my relationship with F1. I'm in love again.

All in all, I think it's a good time to have made that move 'across', as it were. As a driver, the racing had become predictable, whereas as an observer it remains fascinating. You can appreciate the enormous talent of, say, Lewis. You can pick up on the nuances, how certain cars suit certain people. You can enjoy the narrative, the little stories of the weekend.

How will the sport change? I'm not sure that it will. Certainly not in the short term. Mercedes build engines, which they supply to other teams, but they keep the best ones for themselves. The only team with a chance of beating them is another manufacturer team, and right now that's only Ferrari. Still, there are other ways in which the sport can improve. The racing has to be better. If you look at other formulas, the cars don't look as good as F1 cars, they're 12 seconds a lap slower, but the racing's great. There's so much overtaking.

So if you applied that to Formula One, what if they were 10 seconds slower, had less aerodynamics and more mechanical grip? There would be more overtaking.

So reduce downforce. That would be my first change if I were made king of the sport. Next thing, ditch DRS, because it means that everyone waits for the straight to overtake. If there's a possibility of making a move two corners before the straight, you don't take it because you might damage the car and you know you're going to overtake in two corners' time when you're on the straight. Ergo: no risks. People forget that mistakes are an integral part of the sport and again something you inevitably find more entertaining as an observer than you do when you're a part of it. And it's a fact that teams don't make mistakes like they used to. Cars are much more reliable than in the past. You have two Mercedes at the front who are the quickest, who rarely make mistakes. How do you beat them? You don't. The only thing you can do is challenge them knowing that as soon as they feel challenge and competition then *that* is when they'll make mistakes.

Mistakes, then. More overtaking. More action. The most important thing is that the racing is good for fans. And as someone who's now more of a fan than a participant, I'll get behind any measure that does that – as long as it involves ditching DRS.

3. HOW TO REFLECT ON A RACING LIFE

If there's one philosophy that you take away from this, it's Always Be Learning. It's easy to say you should learn through your mistakes, but to put it into practice is something very different.

What have I learnt about myself? Well, for a start, I've learnt that there are certain things I can't change about the way I am, even though I've tried, and one of those is getting over a bad weekend. However much people tell me after a bad race, 'Deal with it, get over it and move on', and however many times I tell myself the same thing, it doesn't change and won't, because that's my weakness – I can't just leave things behind.

So I've learnt that about myself. I've also learnt that there are a lot of sharks in Formula One. I've learnt that it's a fickle business and if you don't come in and you don't perform, you're straight out the door – career over. I've learnt that if you really spend time with quality people in the sport, like the mechanics, you gain a lot of friends and when you win together, it means a lot more than when you win alone. When you're winning with great people around you, it's what it's all about.

When the old man passed away what struck me was a sense of not knowing what life has in store for you. I began to think about how we should take the positives from the past, but always be living in the moment, not worrying about what's happened or what's up next.

Back in the old days, I'd be doing something fun, swimming in the sea in Monaco or mucking about with my mates, driving nice cars, but I'd be thinking, *What am I going to do later? Where are we going to tonight?* But why? Why don't we just enjoy what we're doing right now because what we're doing is awesome.

And I really do believe that now, I think that living in the moment is key to a better life. And all of that is a result of finally, at last, becoming a proper person, not just a selfish bastard. And I guess that's meeting Brit, and becoming a father.

What will fatherhood mean for my driving? Well, in racing they say that a baby is two-tenths. I don't know if that's true because I know a lot of drivers who have kids who haven't slowed down, and as for me, I certainly don't intend to slow down. What I fully expect to experience is a tremendous sense of perspective, a reminder that racing, while important, is just a sport. It's about going out and having fun. And given that new-found perspective maybe I'll be driving better – perhaps it'll ease the pressure. I'll be going out there and enjoying myself.

Ten years back I wouldn't have thought that way. I wasn't ready to be a father then because I was so focused on Formula One. Now I realise that there are things in life that are so much more important than racing and being on the podium. Those moments are great, and I treasure them and I can sit on the sofa with our little boy and go, 'Look, that's your dad, that's when he used to win trophies and dress in his own giant onesie without pockets…'

Most likely his aspirations and interests will be totally different from mine. Whatever they are I'll have his back. But, of course, if it's driving, that's great. Who knows? Maybe I'll get him interested in racing the way my dad did for me – and I'll be the guy in an eye-catching shirt that he's picking out when he sprays his winner's champagne.

We'll see.

ACKNOWLEDGEMENTS

As with everything, there's a big team of people behind the scenes who have made this book possible, from the people who were on this journey with me to those that worked on the book itself. The wonderful Andrew Holmes, Matt Phillips and the team at Blink, David Luxton, team JB and, of course, my incredible family and friends – thank you all so much for the roles you've played and your ongoing support, it means more than you'll ever know.

The final thank you goes, of course, to the sensational future Mrs Button. Brittny, thank you, as always, for your unwavering love, support and understanding with this project, and with everything. Hendrix and I are so lucky to have you, I love you very much.

INDEX

(Page numbers in **bold** refer to significant subject mentions)

INDEX